Memories of the

Rare Old Times

A Dubliner recounts generations of

family life in Ireland

Bernard P Morgan

First published in 2008
© Copyright 2008
Bernard P. Morgan

The right of Bernard P. Morgan to be identified as the author of this work has been asserted by him in accordance with Copyright, Designs and Patents Act 1998. All rights reserved. No reproduction, copy or transmission of these publications may be made without written permission.
No paragraph of this publication may be reproduced, copied or transmitted save with the written permission or in accordance with the provisions of the Copyright Act 1956 (as amended). Any person who does any unauthorized act in relation to this publication may be liable to criminal prosecution and civil claims for damage.

ISBN 9781904312454

MX Publishing Ltd, 335 Princess Park Manor,
Royal Drive, London, N11 3GX
www.mxpublishing.co.uk

I dedicate this book to my beloved brothers and sisters, alive and dead. Growing up with you all was an adventure full of fun and love. To my parents and grandparents, thank you.

And last but not least, to my beloved wife Jennifer and our three wonderful children, Angela, John and Brian.

Memories of the Rare Old Times

Dear Reader,

This book is fiction and fact; I will leave it up to the reader to discern which. The names have been changed for all the characters except Bang-Bang, Razor Throat and Johnnie Forty Coats. I would emphasize that these were lovable characters and in no way would I besmirch their character, this goes for all the players in this book. I don't know all of the personal history of these characters I can only relate my experiences with them. To the people of Dublin: your good nature and charity towards the underdog is legend, and I am proud to be a part of this wonderful city.

I do hope you enjoy reading this book as I have written it with love and memories of you all.

A special thanks to Rosalind Stefanac-Skugor and Jessica Pulis whose help and editing were well received also to Ted Smith who some years ago inspired me to write.

Thank you all.

INTRODUCTION

This book attempts to explain the average family life in Dublin from the early 1900s to the middle '60s. The reader will be introduced to some characters such as Johnny Forty Coats who wore vest, coats and scarves to ward off the cold, no matter what the weather. Bang-Bang was another lovable character who would jump on the buses in and around Dublin shooting at everyone with a large key. He was well loved throughout the city and would turn up in the most unexpected places, which only added to his mystic. The children of Dublin were either terrified of him or loved him. Another character was Razor Throat who used to hold his hand to his neck all of the time, the most harmless of them all. There was also a harsh reality to life in Dublin in the early years. What we take for granted now and what "was" has no comparison, but hardship builds character and

God knows I have met many characters. In all my dealings with Dublin people, no matter what their troubles, in health or death, there was always a wry humour to their demeanor which made light of their troubles. Today, when I return home for a visit I see how Dublin has changed and I am sad to say not for the better. The petty troubles teenagers caused in my youth seem now to be much more violent. However, Dublin is still a very safe city to visit and I would not for one moment deter anyone from visiting. I have had the honour and pleasure of knowing some of the best people on earth and will always be grateful to have known them and all the friends of my childhood because I remember "The Rare old Times." I think this poem best describes the Irish. It was given to me by my friend Bob Bulger, the most decent and likeable individual you could hope to meet. It's beautiful and titled, *The Irish.* The author remains unknown.

THE IRISH

WHAT SHALL I SAY ABOUT THE IRISH....?

THE: UTTERLY, IMPRACTICAL, NEVER PREDICTABLE SOMETIMES IRASCIBLE, QUITE INEXPLICABLE IRISH: STRANGE BLEND OF SHYNESS, PRIDE AND CONCEIT, AND STUBBORN REFUSAL TO BOW IN DEFEAT. HE'S SPOILING AND READY TO ARGUE AND FIGHT, YET THE SMILE OF A CHILD FILLS HIS SOUL WITH DELIGHT. HIS EYES ARE THE QUICKEST TO WELL UP WITH TEARS, YET HIS STRENGTH IS THE STRONGEST TO BANISH YOUR FEARS HIS HATE IS AS FIERCE AS HIS DEVOTION IS GRAND, AND THERE'S NO MIDDLE GROUND ON WHICH HE WILL STAND. HE'S WILD AND HE'S GENTLE HE'S GOOD AND HE'S BAD, HE'S PROUD AND HE'S HUMBLE, HE'S HAPPY AND SAD. HE'S IN LOVE WITH THE OCEAN, THE EARTH AND THE SKIES, HE'S ENAMORED WITH BEAUTY WHEREVER IT LIES. HE'S VICTOR AND VICTIM, A STAR AND A CLOD, BUT MOSTLY HE'S IRISH....IN LOVE WITH HIS GOD.

CHAPTER 1

He was a sickly child when he entered the world in 1942. His mother was poorly but she would survive. This boy was her 9th. Bugs her husband came into the ward asking, "Well Maggie what is it this time?" "It's a boy she answered but I don't think he is well," she replied..." Bugs walked over to the crib, "Jeeze Maggie he's an ugly bastard, who's the father?" he asked -- Bang Bang.

A smile came to Maggie's face as she looked at Bugs with his receding hairline, broken nose and missing teeth. Better to say nothing, she thought, for he was really a kind man. She thought back to her youth when she had first met Joe, alias Bugs, on Aaron Quay. He was 20 and she was 17. He was so handsome then in his Free Irish Uniform and he had whistled as she passed him. Her friend Mary Irons said "Ignore him Maggie," but she turned and smiled at him. He winked and went on his way.

It was one year later that Maggie met Joe again. It was New Year's Eve at Christchurch in the center of Dublin. The dance was just finishing and Joe was arguing with a policeman on the corner. Joe suddenly punched the man in the face; he crumpled to the ground, blood pouring from his nose. Joe walked away down Christchurch hill and that's when Maggie saw the paddy wagon pull up beside Joe. A sergeant jumped out and hit Joe across the back with his truncheon; another policeman kicked him in the side. Maggie screamed and ran to his aid hitting the sergeant on the head with her umbrella. Joe was on his feet by now and, butting the sergeant in the face, he turned and caught the other policeman flush on the chin. Both men were down, Joe turned and smiled at Maggie, "Well young lady we should get away from here." They both ran down the hill.

"Where do you live?" he asked. "I live in Bow Street," Maggie replied. "But don't you remember me?" "I do, your name is Maggie Hennesey. You have three brothers named Paddy, Dick and Ritchie. One is a horse cab driver, the other is in the British army and Ritchie works for the corporation. Of course I remember you you're always in my thoughts." Maggie looked at Joe in complete surprise. She thought from their first encounter that Joe had forgotten her but it turns out he had not.

They walked together up Cook Street and crossed the road to Oliver Bond House. It was a very tough part of Dublin but everyone they passed seemed to know Bugs. Maggie had still wondered how he knew her brothers and now she understood. She asked Joe where he came from and he related this story. "I'm from the Falls Road, Belfast. I had to leave my family, job and friends because of those Black and Tan bastards. They hunted me out over a silly argument." Joe went on to explain how he was in a pub in Belfast with his mates when eight Black and Tans walked in banging their nightsticks trying to push the crowd into a fight. There had been complete silence in the bar as the customers looked at the Tans with hatred in their eyes. Joe's mate Paddy Maher had lifted his pint to take a drink when one of the Tans broke it with his night stick scattering glass and Guinness everywhere and started the fight Belfast never forgot. Mick Flynn, a small stocky man who was an acquaintance of Joe, kicked the Tan in the balls. His eyeballs nearly popped out. Another Tan clubbed Mick, the remainder joined in beating him over the head. The customers still had not moved. Everybody was thunderstruck as it happened so quickly. John McGuire, a seaman who was on leave from the merchant navy, and another mate of Bugs' threw a chair and hit a Tan on the face breaking his jaw. Pandemonium broke out. Bugs standing 6'1" and solid as a rock, punched all in front of him. Teeth were flying, chairs and tables scattered. The barman who weighed about 300 lbs ran from behind the bar, shouting "Gentlemen stop this madness!" before he too to was thrown out of the large plate glass window on the door of the pub, falling unconscious on the welcome mat in front, where two soldiers threw him into an army truck. Ten more soldiers came out of a truck parked outside and entered the melee. By this time there were a lot of Tans and some customers were hurt very badly. Bugs and John were cornered, fighting off four Tans, clubs were swinging, when suddenly John pulled a knife and stabbed a Tan in the chest. The fighting took on a deadly earnest. One Tan at the back of the room drew his pistol and started shooting. A stray bullet penetrated the wooden partition of the snug were Mary O'Hara was sitting and she fell dead with a bullet in her chest. More of the Tans pulled their guns and the owner of pub was shot in the face shattering his jaw. A sergeant took control of the crowd by firing shots into the air and telling them to surrender before there were any more deaths. The fighting stopped and all the customers were lined up at the bar, women and men in separate groups. The women where then told to leave. They had to pass a line of Tans outside the pub and as they ran crying from the scene they were pushed and punched. Sixteen of the customers where then marched out and into the awaiting army trucks and driven to a barracks outside of Belfast. The Tan who had been killed and the barman still unconscious were put into a truck and driven away. Joe still stunned over what had happened was in a small cell in the army Barracks. His head was pounding and with his hand throbbing, he thought it must be broken. His thoughts then turned to the picture of Mary O'Hara lying in the snug in a pool of blood. Her family would be devastated. Why did this happen? England is the most democratic country on earth, but when it came to Northern Ireland it was blind. Most recruits for the Black and Tans were of low character. England emptied its prisons for their recruits. He thought of all the Irishmen that had died for England in wars with foreign powers. Why was there so much discrimination of the Catholic population with housing, jobs and schools? You could deal with the British army but the

Tans were the scourge of Ireland.

The cell door suddenly burst open and water from a hose hit Joe in the face knocking him off his cot. "You bastards," he screamed, as the cell shut just as quickly. The cold did not bother him for a while, but as the hours passed he began to understand what his time in the barracks would really be like. He finally fell asleep dreaming of Mary covered in blood. He awoke with a start as the cell door opened. He was given some sort of gruel and tea and the door quickly slammed shut again. Joe tried to eat his breakfast but his hand was very swollen and trembling. It was about noon when the sergeant of the Tans opened his cell door. Joe complained about his hand. "Feck your hand," he replied. "You should have thought of your hand last night." "Sod you," Joe replied. "If you blokes were not looking for trouble, none of this would have happened.

Two people are dead because of you." The sergeant went to hit Joe but thought better of it as Joe stood up. "Try it," Joe said, "or do you need more back up?" The sergeant glared at Joe. "If you didn't have to go before the magistrate it would give me great pleasure." "Really," Joe said. "I was wondering how you got your pleasure." With that the sergeant left and banged the cell shut behind him.

Sometime later Joe was taken from his cell and down to the infirmary to have his hand examined. The doctor came in and looked it over carefully. "You have had a bad sprain but you will be okay," he said. The nurse wrapped Joe's hand and gave him a sedative. As he was sitting waiting to be brought back to his cell he saw Mick Flynn lying on a bed across from him. His head was bandaged and his eyes swollen shut. "Mick how are you?" Mick opened one eye and smiled. "I'm fine Joe, just a bit groggy. It will take more than those bastards to put me down."

"That's the spirit my old mate," Joe replied. "Would you get word to my family Joe and tell them what happened or my wife will think I'm off drinking somewhere." A guard came into the infirmary to take Joe back to his cell. "Take care Mick, chin up I'11 see you soon." As he was led back to his cell Joe was concentrating on how to escape from this place, it seemed impregnable but somehow he had to find a way or those bastards would probably charge him with murder. He thought of John McGuire stabbing that Tan. What a fool he was. Joe had never used a weapon in a fight in his life. He had not even known John had a knife, but who would believe him. As they were passing the kitchen, he spotted on old neighbor, Bill Taft, mopping the floors. Bill spotted Joe but gave no inkling that he had recognized him.

Joe was put into a larger cell with a toilet and washbasin. I must be here for longer than I expected, he thought. As the guard shut the cell door, he threw Joe a pack of cigarettes and matches. "Don't burn yourself and keep them hidden," he said. Joe was astonished by this gesture. He must be Catholic he thought to himself and smiled. "Thanks mate," Joe replied. As the guard turned to walk down the corridor Joe shouted after him, "Could you find out if my father and mother have been told of my trouble?" "I'll do my best," was the reply. Joe looked around the cell. What a miserable hole he thought. It was dark and dingy and there was a bad aura about this prison, but he had to pull himself together.

Joe settled down in his cell pondering his troubles and knowing that he had to get away. But where? England? Maybe. He would be able to get lost in London but they would be watching the ships. He also had no money but first things first. He had to get out of these army barracks. He heard footsteps in the corridor, cell doors opening and rattling of the tin plates, dinnertime. He heard voices and suddenly realized his mates from the pub where in the other cells. Five minutes later his cell door opened and Bill Taft from the kitchen was serving the meal. "Hello Joe, and what have you been up to this time?" he asked. "Hello Bill, just a little fight that got out of hand. Could you get word to my family and tell them where I am?" "I will Joe, when I finish my shift. But for God's sake watch out for Sergeant Tom McIvor. He's a real demon, so don't cross him. Eat this dinner. You'll need all of your strength in this place. I'11 see you tomorrow." With that he closed the cell door. Joe felt a lot better now that he had seen a friend. He ate heartily. It was some sort of stew, but food was food. He was wondering who sergeant Tom McIvor was. He had seen an evil-looking person pass his cell, never saying a word. Hopefully it wasn't him, Joe pondered.

Later on that night someone from the cell across from his whispered, "Joe is that you? It's me Ernie Hickey." Ernie was the milkman in Joe's district. He was one of the most prim and proper men Joe had ever known, never in trouble and as neat as a pin. Now here he was in bits in a prison cell. Joe was smiling as he replied "Yes it's me. How are you Ernie?" "Jeeze Joe I feel like shit. I can't eat my food because I lost two teeth. I was ugly before this but jeeze Joe, you should see me now.

My girlfriend will leave me for sure; I only went in for a pint before I took Marie to the pictures. She was waiting for me downtown. We were having trouble before this happened; now I think this is it." Joe was smiling as Ernie rattled on. "Joe I didn't even get to punch one of those bastards. I threw a punch at this little bloke, thought I couldn't miss him, when all of a sudden he ducked and his fists were flying in every direction. He must have been the fecking boxing champion of Britain. I will probably be fired from my job. I will lose my girlfriend, and as the sergeant was throwing me in my cell, he said "I will see you later you hooligan." Me, who never caused trouble in my life. That was it for Joe who could not contain his laughter any longer. He fell off his bunk onto his knees and it was some minutes later when he regained his composure. "Joe, Joe, what's the matter, are you sick?" Ernie asked. Again, Joe started laughing.

"I'm okay and you will be all right, just be quiet and get some sleep," he told Ernie. Joe slept well that night. He awoke at 7 a.m. to the sounds of breakfast being served; the aroma of porridge penetrated his cell. Bill opened his cell door. "I went to your house; you're breaking your mother's heart." He took some cigarettes from his pocket and handed them to Joe. Your brother sent them to you. "Bill, can you help me get out of this place?" Joe pleaded. "Joe I'll be shot if I do that. I heard what happened and I know you blokes were pushed into that fight. I'll help you get out, but don't escape on my shift." Joe was elated when Bill suggested Thursday as the sergeant goes away every Thursday. "I'll arrange for your brothers to be outside. For now eat your breakfast. I can't be seen talking to you," he said. What a break, Joe thought, but where would he go? It had to be

Dublin. He would be safe there. The thought of leaving his job and family hung heavy on Joe for the remainder of the night and with a sad heart he awoke the next day.

It was Monday. Three more days and he would escape. He lay back on his bunk listening to the sounds of the army barracks, and the day passed quickly. A soldier served his dinner this time and he wondered if everything was all right with Bill. He slept fitfully that night waking at 4 a.m. Not a sound to be heard, he lit a cigarette and thought of the events that had brought him here. He could have passed the pub. He should have gone home. He was still daydreaming when he heard the breakfast trays banging and it seemed like an eternity before his cell door finally opened. Bill walked in. "Thank God it's you, where have you been? asked Joe. "Be quiet, I have some news for you. The court hearing is Thursday morning, I heard about it yesterday. Joe, that sergeant Tom McIvor has it in for you. Be prepared to leave tonight as the Barracks will be almost empty and the men are going on overnight maneuvers. I will leave the door of your cell open before I finish my shift. There is a janitor's cupboard at the top of the stairs. Oh never mind, I will draw a map."

"Bill why are you going to all this trouble to help me?" Joe asked "We weren't exactly friends." "You are lucky this is not Crumlin Road Jail which is a lot harder to escape from. If you are wondering why I am helping you Joe—me a Protestant and you a Catholic—I will tell you. My son Tony had an accident in England on a construction site. He was badly injured. He is my only son and was in a sanitarium outside Manchester. His mother and I went over as often as we could to see him but he was a long time mending and money was very short. The only kindness we were shown was from your Mom and Dad. Everyday they came to our house with a hot meal as my wife was devastated. One morning I came down and there was an envelope at my front door with 10 shillings in it, and this went on for some weeks; it was a Godsend. To cut a long story short, I stayed up and watched my front door and I saw your dad Liam push an envelope in my letter box. I rushed down and opened the door. "What's going on Liam?" I demanded. Your father was taken aback. Why are you doing this? You can't afford it with your big family. His only reply was you're a neighbor and I'm getting a bit of extra work. Jeeze Joe, I'm Protestant he's a Catholic. I was shocked. I love that man and that's why I'm helping you Tony never recovered from his injuries but I've got nothing to lose and even if I had, I would still help you."

Joe looked at Bill and thought of his father. He never knew he has helped Bill and his family. Joe was contemplating the story he had just heard and he felt very sorry for Bill. He had heard that his son had died in England but had never given it much thought. "The only people who were at my son's funeral in England were your Mom, Dad, the minister, my wife and me. I don't know if I would have kept my sanity without your parent's support. Whatever you do, follow the directions I give you when I serve your lunch." With that Bill shut the cell door.

Joe had a wash at the sink. His luck was changing He had to leave Belfast, that was certain. He was deep in thought when he heard lunch being served. Bill entered his cell. "Well Joe I finish my shift soon. The map is under your lunch tray. Follow the directions carefully and God bless you. I will unlock your cell before I leave, be careful," he said and left. An hour or so later as Joe was lying on his cot, the cell door opened and Tom McIver was standing glaring at Joe. "Your court case is in a few days and when you return from court I will deal with you." With that he banged the cell door shut and was gone. Joe shouted. "Feck off, you evil bastard."

Joe read the map. He was on the ground floor of the barracks. He was to hide in the closet at the end of the corridor until 8 p.m. everything would be quiet by then. Suddenly a thought flashed through his mind. He realized Bill could not leave his cell door open as the guard would find the cell unlocked when they served dinner. What a mix up, he thought. The hours went by slowly until dinner time Then Bill entered the cell and before Joe could confront him with the news, Bill said: "I know Joe, I was not thinking straight but I will be here after dinner. I usually play cards with old Billy who is on watch at night. I will find some way of opening your cell door." Relief spread across Joe's face. "Jeeze Bill, I nearly had heart failure," he said. They both smiled. When Bill left Joe slept, he wanted to be ready as he knew he would not be sleeping for a while. Dinner was served. He ate slowly and read the map again. He was to make his way downstairs to the back of the cells, crossing the field and keeping away from the main entrance. He was engrossed in thought when he heard the cell door being unlocked. "Good luck," Bill whispered. It was an eternity before everything was quiet. He stuffed his bunk as best he could to make believe he was asleep if the guard looked in.

He then made his way to the cupboard, entered and made himself comfortable for the wait. He left two hours later and followed the directions on the map. He was making his way across the field when two Black and Tans came walking past. He dropped onto his stomach instantly and they passed without seeing him. Joe stayed on the grass for another ten minutes then scaled the wall. It was a pitch black night which he was thankful for. He soon found himself on a country road and made his way in the opposite direction to the camp. There was coal truck parked on the road. He walked to the opposite side when a voice whispered, "Is that you Joe?" His brother Tom was in the truck. "Thank God it's you, we haven't much time Joe. I have to get this truck back to the yard before it's missed. I am going to drop you as near as I can to the border. There are some clothes for you to change as we drive," he said, and with that they started on the journey. They drove to the border without mishap. Tom pulled over at a safe distance from the check point. "Joe there is a bike on the back of the truck. Here is some money, sorry it is not more." He handed Joe a five-pound note. "Get word to us of where you will be staying in Dublin and the family will try and get to see you. There were tears in Tom's eyes as they embraced. "Be careful Joe and God bless you."

Joe cycled for about half a mile, and then spotting some soldiers on guard duty he walked his bike making a very wide circle and being very quiet until he was out of sight. He lifted his bike over a fence and had a grueling walk through some very muddy fields.

Eventually he made it to a country lane. It was one of the most exhausting journeys Joe had ever made. He did most of his traveling at night. He eventually arrived in Dublin, cold, tired and hungry. His first priority was to clean himself up and join the Irish Army. This was all accomplished on his first day there.

"Well Maggie," he said, "That's my life story." It was 2 a.m. by this time and Joe and Maggie where standing on Queen Street Bridge. Maggie said, "That was a very sad story and I'm sorry you had to leave your family and friends Joe." Maggie realized what time it was and said, "For God's sake Joe get me home or else my mother will kill me! Where has the time gone?" They both made their way up Queen Street, cutting across Smithfield when two MPs called to them. "Get in Joe, you are in trouble again," one of them said. Joe turned to Maggie. "You will be safe now. I will get word to you as soon as possible. I am stationed at Collin's Barracks," he said, and with that he was driven off. Maggie turned into Bow Street. What an unusual man. I'm going to marry Joe Moran someday, she thought as she turned the key and entered her house.

CHAPTER 2

Maggie's mother was standing in the kitchen arms folded and clearly upset. "Do you know what time it is?" she shouted. "No decent lady keeps these hours. Do you want your reputation to be destroyed? If your father were here you would not be doing this." "Why is my father not here?" Maggie shouted back. With that her mother started to cry, he should be with you, Maggie thought, but it is impossible. Maggie knew that her father had to leave Dublin because of some trouble with the police, but she never knew the reason. She was bitter towards him for deserting her when she was just seven years of age. Her mother went on to explain. "Your father lives in Scotland, just outside of Glasgow. He sends money when he can and he loves his family. Sit by the fire Maggie dear and I will make you something to eat." When they were both comfortable her mother began to tell Maggie the story of why her father had to leave Dublin.

Maggie's father was born in Smithfield, Dublin. Years ago it was used as a trading centre for the buying and selling of horses. It was surrounded in the heart of Dublin by quaint terraced houses. The British army was in occupation at this time. These were hard times in Dublin and people made a living any way they could. Paddy Hennesey was a very proud man, even arrogant at times, but a good provider and a staunch friend when the need arose. As he was growing up in Dublin, England occupied half the world, including Ireland. The Irish language was banned in the schools, the Irish police were strongly influenced by the British and a lot of hatred for the police was generated by this situation, causing Paddy trouble in later years. There were thirteen children in Paddy's family, nine brothers and four sisters, it was a hard and poor upbringing. He left school when he was thirteen to work as a messenger boy for the daily newspaper, which helped with the family budget. Over the years he was in the usual trouble of a teenager. At eighteen he joined the British army, like many Irishmen during these times. It was either unemployment or the service. He was sent to Aldershot in England for his basic training, and then sent to the Middle East, where he soon got into the routine of army life. His money was sent home to his family on a regular basis. In all the skirmishes in the Middle East, Paddy distinguished himself on the battlefield, rising to the rank of sergeant and was discharged six years later. He roamed England for a year or two then decided to go home to Dublin. There were quite a few English firms in Dublin so Paddy had no trouble finding a job especially with his army record. Life was boring for him after the excitement of army life and he started drinking with his old mates, fighting in the bars of Dublin, and getting into trouble with the police, especially with a corporal named Joe O'Shea. On one particular night Paddy was in a fight outside a bar in Kingsbridge - a major train station in Dublin. The police were called out to stop the fight as there were quite a few injuries among the combatants and nine of them including Paddy were sentenced to six months in Mount Joy. That is where he first met Maggie's mother Catherine who worked for the prison services as a nurse. It was love at first sight when Catherine saw Paddy. He stood six feet tall with the broadest shoulders she had ever seen. Catherine was five feet tall with the reddest hair he had ever seen. When Paddy finished his sentence they were married three months later, much to the dismay of Catherine's family. They went to live in a small house in Lucan just outside of Dublin and these were very happy years for the two of them until he lost his job and they returned to Dublin along with their three sons. Luck was with them again as Paddy managed to get a job on the Dublin docks. He worked hard and settled into the routine of family life. Soon after this Maggie was born, he was besotted with his beautiful daughter. As the years passed Paddy was promoted to checker - a person who is responsible for the cargo entering the docks.

Life was good for the family, with a nice house and a few extras with his increase in pay. In those days when you worked on the docks you put a shilling in a matchbox and gave it to your foreman, to ensure your name was picked when a ship arrived to unload. There were a lot more men than was needed and the men did what they could for work with the addition of an extra person their house did not seem big enough and they moved to a three-bedroom house on Bow Street. Leading up the 1916 Rebellion there was unrest between the British Army and the IRA. Paddy's local pub was on the corner of Smithfield and Queen Street and he used to go out every night for a few pints. On one particular night, Paddy was there with his friend Liam Fagan when he had a second run in with Corporal Joe O' Shea.

Joe was from county Sligo. He had lived in Dublin for fifteen years where he was employed by the police. He was very pro British like most of the force, and was well known for his harassment of the people in the district. Joe was also a noted amateur boxer. When he arrested someone, whether it was for stealing, drunkenness or fighting, he gave them an alternative: fight him one on one or go to the cells. The poor sods usually agreed to fight him as they could not afford to go to jail. They could be there for a week to a month before their cases were heard. Of course Joe used to beat the poor sods silly.

There was a character the locals called "Gunner Eye" since his eyes were not aligned properly. He was a gentle man when sober but when drunk he was one of the most obnoxious people you could meet—a right knowledgeable asshole. He knew everything and knew nothing. The locals loved him and used to tease him to get him annoyed. When he went to the toilets he used to take his false teeth out and put them in his pint so it would not be taken. The odd time the blokes in the bar would empty his pint and put the teeth back into the empty glass. On one particular occasion when the blokes had done this, Johnny Forty Coats came into the bar to bum a drink. Johnny was a Dublin character who used to wear coats, scarves, sweaters, all covered with a great army coat, come rain or snow. He was a lovable character who would do no harm. He slept rough in the local park and used to get hand-outs from the local merchants. Gunner Eye came out of the toilet and found his glass empty with his false teeth at the bottom. He ran down the bar shouting, "Who the Feck took my drink?" He was ranting and raving that he would fight the hardest man in the pub because he was not one to be trifled with. By now everyone was laughing which only infuriated him more. They were still teasing him when he spotted Johnny Forty Coats.

Gunner Eye went up to Johnny. "Where's my pint?" he asked. Johnny replied "I will have a glass of Guinness." "No," Gunner Eye shouted. "Buy me the pint that you stole from me." The people in the bar were flabbergasted. "I did not steal your pint but I will have glass of Guinness and if you could spare the odd shilling, God bless you," said Johnny." By now Gunner Eye was shaking with temper. "You idiot," he shouted. "Buy me a pint or I will stick one on you." With that Johnny Forty coats punched him on the nose and knocked him down. Johnny then ran out of the pub. It was done so quickly that everyone was silenced for a few seconds before laughter rang out. Gunner Eye got up from the floor "Where's that bastard?" he shouted, which caused more laughter. He was going to search Dublin for Johnny Forty Coats and when he found him he was going to thrash him within one inch of his life.

As he was running about the bar shouting, he bumped into Joe O'Shea. Joe was in a foul mood and caught Gunner Eye by the back of the neck. "Who are you pushing Stupid?" Everyone was enjoying the spectacle at Gunner Eyes expense, but now they grew quiet as they all knew Joe O'Shea. Gunner Eye shouted at Joe, "Let me go or I will thrash you." Everyone smiled, even Joe. Relief came over their faces and Joe said to Gunner Eye, "I'm sorry if you are upset." Everyone relaxed, when all of a sudden Gunner Eye butted Joe who looked at him with murder in his eyes and hit Gunner across his face with his night stick knocking him out. Liam Fagan shouted, "What the Feck did you do that for?" Joe ran and whacked Liam and when Paddy saw Liam go down, he punched Joe across the head. Joe fell to one knee and looked up to see Paddy standing over him. "You are under arrest," he said to

Paddy. "You are the one who should be arrested not me." With that Joe jumped up and hit Paddy across the head with his night stick. Paddy had never been hit so hard before. He was dazed and he could not stand straight. By this time more policemen had arrived and arrested the whole bar. Everyone had started fighting just for the fun of it.

The next morning Paddy awoke in the cells of the local police station, Bridewell, with the most terrible headache. He was with Liam Fagan and a few other bar patrons including Gunner Eye. He looked around the cell. It was like a war zone, with everyone suffering bloody cuts and black eyes. It was a funny sight except for Gunner Eye who seemed to have come out of the melee worst of all. "Paddy what happened to me? I feel really bad," said Gunner." There was a significant slur in his voice and everyone was smiling even in their pain. Gunner Eye continued, "Who is the bowsie that hit me? If I had have seen him coming I would have given him the beating of his life." Gunner Eye was seven stone and could not beat a fly. Paddy was wondering if Catherine was okay and not worrying about him. He dozed for a while and awoke with a start as the cell doors opened. "Wake up you slieveens," said the guard. "Get on home and don't be starting fights again. You were lucky this time but next time you won't be." Paddy and his friends left the Bridewell station and as Paddy was walking down the lane when he was accosted by Joe O'Shea. "You got off easy you Fenian bastard and I'm here to remedy that," he said as he made a swing at Paddy. Thoughts of Joe hitting Gunner Eye in the face with his night stick flooded Paddy's mind as he very quickly stepped aside and caught Joe across the side of the head sending him banging against the wall. All the commotion brought some policemen on the scene and they went to get Paddy when Joe staggered to his feet. "Leave him be and let him go, I will deal with this bastard later." Paddy walked away quickly as he seemed to have a feud on with this egomaniac. I will keep a low profile, he thought.

Paddy's life soon got back to normal and he never gave Joe O'Shea a second thought. He was doing well in his job on the docks and the following year he was promoted to foreman. The extra money allowed Paddy and Catherine to live a little better and life was good. One Sunday the whole of his family was walking in the Phoenix Park. It was a beautiful day and the kids were playing soccer. A group of men came walking by when suddenly one of them left the group and approached Paddy. "So there you are you bastard." Joe O' Shea was glaring at Paddy with hatred in his eyes. "Are you ready to fight now?" asked Joe. Paddy said, "Can't you see I am with my family, have you no respect for the Sabbath." "You have an excuse for every occasion not to face me," replied Joe. "I will fight you any place you pick, win or lose, as long as there is an end to this," said Joe. They both glared at each other. Catherine was shaking with fright. She did not know what was going on but she knew hatred when she saw it. Paddy thought, "Here I am minding my own business, having a nice day out with my family when this person filled with vindictiveness picks on me in front of my family." "Give me two hours and I will meet you at Island Street just off Oliver Bond House", he whispered to Joe. "Agreed," he replied.

Paddy rushed his family home. He was shaking with rage and could not wait to get to Island Street. He would teach this arrogant bastard a lesson. Paddy trotted across Smithfield, up Queen Street, and across Queen Street Bridge. As he approached Island Street his adrenaline was pumping. When he turned the corner from Bridgefoot Street there was a large crowd waiting. News traveled fast in this town, thought Paddy. Joe had not arrived yet. It was now early afternoon. Somewhere in the crowd the locals were taking bets. Most were banking on Joe O'Shea to win as his reputation as a fighter was solid. An hour passed and the crowd was becoming restless when all of a sudden along came Joe and his pal in civvies. A murmur went through the crowd. "Where were you cowardly bastard?" someone shouted from the crowd. "Sorry I'm late," Joe replied. "I had to teach one of you bastards a lesson. I arrested him for answering me back." With that the crowd hissed. Jim McEvoy from Pimlico, (a district in Dublin) shouted at the bloke who was taking bets, "Change my bet, I'm for Paddy." With that the entire crowd changed their bets. "Paddy was elated when the crowd rooted for him, for in his heart he knew that he would win. After all, he was a spring ready to be released. There were shouts of "good luck Paddy" from the crowd. "If this bloke wins this fight I will be dead," Paddy replied. With this a cheer went up through the crowd. By now there was a large ring of people around Joe and Paddy. Someone in the crowd took it upon themselves to be the referee. "Here are the rules gentlemen," he stated, "when a man is unconscious the fight ends. Now go to your respective corners."

Joe looked at Paddy who was now stripped to the waist. His years in the army and on the docks had left him with a very powerful build. Joe thought to himself that this was a man that he would have to be very careful with. As they were watching each other, Joe tried to rile Paddy. By now the crowd had increased and there was a large ring around the combatants. Joe had landed the first punch and rocked Paddy, cutting the side of his lip where a little blood now trickled down the side of his mouth. Again Joe landed a punch, all of the time insulting Paddy.

"Fight you Fenian bastard," shouted Joe. His training in the ring was paying off for Paddy was swinging wildly and missing each time. With every punch that Joe landed, the crowd groaned. "Come on Paddy," McEvoy shouted but Paddy was getting bashed. He was worried now. He was not hurting because his adrenaline was pumping and all he wanted was to knock the smirk off O'Shea's face. He was so full of disgust for this person that he would take every punch that Joe landed just to get one back.

By now Paddy's face was a bit of a mess but he was beginning to know Joe's weakness. As Paddy threw a punch, Joe's head went to the left, so when Paddy threw the next punch he feigned a punch to Joe's left side and caught him right on the chin. Joe's head exploded as he went down. He was punched a lot in his time but never like this. Immediately he knew that he was in trouble. As he sat on the ground, his pal toweled his face, he eventually sat up and looked around, he was still dizzy but now he looked at Paddy with new respect. The crowd went wild cheering when Paddy hit Joe. McEvoy shouted from the crowd, "How about that punch from a Fenian bastard?" Everyone started laughing. Joe rested for a couple of minutes then stood up to fight again.

This time he was very careful and the fight took on a new intensity. They both hated each other and the punches were becoming more vicious. They were no longer trying to be fancy, but just slugged away at one another. There was a shout to break. Both fighters were relieved as the blood was flowing freely by now. They rested for a couple of minutes, which was a blessing for Paddy who was exhausted. "Are you ready Joe?" Paddy asked. "Sure," Joe replied. It was getting dark and Joe had started to weaken. Paddy's surprising endurance was wearing him down. There was another break called when Paddy asked "Is it finished now?" "Feck you," Joe replied. The fight continued when Paddy hit Joe with a clean punch and Joe went down for the sixth time. Paddy returned to his corner waiting for Joe to recover. By now the fight had traveled from Island Street and Bridgefoot Street to the walls of the River

Liffey. Joe recovered and came again at Paddy this time catching him on the chin. Paddy shook his head and retaliated by punching Joe in the chest. Both men were exhausted when Joe again punched Paddy, who staggered and before he could recover butted Paddy right on the nose. As Paddy fell to the ground, Joe kicked him in the ribs. When this happened the crowed booed, up until this time, it had been a fair fight. Paddy had some water thrown on his face but he was hurting badly. "Had enough yet?" mocked Joe. Paddy just smiled. My God, he thought, I'm not going to make it. They went at it again with Joe still fighting dirty as he knew he could not win this fight clean. Paddy was really mad now and every punch Joe threw Paddy took. Joe was desperate as he was tired and his arms were falling by his sides. Paddy was punching him all over his body until he caught him with one punch to the head that laid him right out. A great cheer rang from the crowd and Paddy was hoisted onto their shoulders. As the bookie was paying out the bets, the police surrounded the crowd. Joe was coming to and was looking around for Paddy. When he spotted him he shouted, "Arrest that bastard for assaulting a police officer." Paddy was infuriated. He ran at Joe and grabbed him by the neck and leg and with his massive strength hoisted Joe above his head and threw him into the River Liffey. Everyone was aghast. There was a great silence until a policeman went to grab Paddy. Someone in the crowd punched the policeman and shouted "Run Paddy." Paddy ran across Queen Street Bridge, his lungs bursting he knew he was in big trouble. He crossed Smithfield and into Bow Street. He eventually made it to his house where Catherine was waiting from him.

Shocked by his appearance she ran to his side. Paddy told her everything that had taken place and was sobbing, "I think I have killed a policeman." They were both crying when they heard a knock at to the door. Liam Fagan was there. "Paddy," he said, "They have pulled Joe O'Shea from the river and he is in a bad way. You will have to leave Ireland; they will hang you if he dies. Even if he recovers you are looking at serving ten years." Catherine started crying again, but she pulled herself together and agreed with Liam that Paddy would have to leave. They gave Paddy all the money they had between them. Paddy kissed Catherine, "I will be in touch" he said. "I'm going to stay with a friend of mind from the East Wall, and I will get word to you when I have made some plans."

The police came every day looking for Paddy. They

were determined to arrest him. Three weeks later as Catherine was walking down Church Street a pal of Paddy's approached her and told her Paddy wanted to see her and the kids in John's Lane chapel. It would be safe there if the police were watching, they would think she would be going to mass. The meeting was to take place the following day. Catherine was up early and she readied the children to meet their father. She had a feeling Paddy would be leaving the country. They arrived at John's Lane mid morning as previously arranged. She looked around but there was no sign of him. He suddenly appeared at the confessionals at the back of the church. Paddy looked at his family and there were tears welling in his eyes, he flung his arms around Catherine as if he would never let her go. "Catherine I will have to leave Dublin, I can't stand the thought of being imprisoned again." Catherine looked at her husband, he was the most decent and kindest man she had every known, her heart was breaking at the thought of living without him. She just smiled at Paddy "I know, we all love you and may God go with you." Paddy was shaking with sorrow. He couldn't stand to look at his beloved family. He turned and walked away out of the side entrance. Catherine and the children sobbed as he disappeared.

There was not a sound in the house but Maggie's sobbing as Catherine finished her story. "I'm sorry Mom I didn't know, and I'm sorry you had to live without him."

Joe O'Shea eventually recovered. Paddy Hennessey died from injuries he received while working in Scotland in a rail yard. He did come back to see

Catherine years before and sent word to her that he wanted to see her. Their daughter Maggie had never forgiven her father for walking out on them. Maggie would not hear of her mum going to meet her dad. "No Mam, he left us when we needed him, please don't go and see him." After waiting for two days, Paddy returned to Scotland without ever seeing his beloved Catherine or children again. In later years Maggie came to realize she had made a terrible mistake and there wasn't a day that passed when she didn't feel a deep sadness for her interference. It was something she often mentioned to her children and later her grandchildren. She never forgave herself.

CHAPTER 3

Maggie twisted and turned all night thinking about Joe and about her father. She did remember a very big and gentle man, but that was all. She wished she could have known his better. She awoke late the next morning and came down for breakfast. Her three brothers and mother were already eating. Her brother Patsy had some good news. He was going to be married to a girl from Pimlico and everyone was excited. Maggie teased him, "Who would marry the likes of you?" He just smiled. "Women find me very attractive and desirable," he said, and with that they all laughed. Catherine carried the joke on by saying, "You are as hard to look at as the sun God help you. When you were a baby I had to keep you hidden for fear your ugliness would blind people. Now be quiet and eat your breakfast," she said. There was more laughter. Mick tried to add on to the humour and said,

"Now if you are talking about good looks, women find me very" before he could finish Catherine jumped in again. "You be quiet because when I hid your brother I used to put him on top of you in the pram and then pile it up with laundry" Maggie was laughing very hard. This is what it was like every day. They were still laughing when Patsy got up from the table. "Excuse me I'm going to shave and give the mirror a treat." Ritchie was sitting there with a smug face when Catherine asked him, "Why are you smiling? I only took you out at night when you were small for fear the circus people would take you for a side show." With that she looked up to heaven in mock exasperation her hands in the air. "Why was I so cursed?" Maggie was still laughing heartily looking at her brothers for they were really handsome, but you never bandy words with Catherine. Maggie finished breakfast and rushed off to work at

Jacobs. Jacobs was a biscuit factory in the heart of Dublin and one of its main employers. Maggie's mom also worked there along with her friend Mary Irons. She was late but she thought of Joe Moran all the way to work. She would ask her friend Mary Irons to accompany her up to Collins Barracks to see Joe. When Maggie arrived for work she approached Mary and told her of her plan to visit Joe at the Barracks. Mary said, "I'm not going with you; you will ruin your life with a person of the likes of him." Maggie was adamant and Mary relented. They made arrangements to visit Joe on the following Saturday. I will invite him to my brother's wedding, Maggie thought. She and Mary planned to meet at the corner of Queen Street Bridge. Mary lived on Arron Quay and Maggie in Bow Street a couple of minutes away from each other. The week dragged by very slowly for Maggie. Her thoughts were always on Joe, and she knew she was falling in love with him. He was the most exciting and interesting man she had ever met. Saturday finally arrived and she met Mary as they had arranged. Mary greeted Maggie. "You're mad to be doing this." They both laughed and started to walk up the Quays to Collins Barracks. Maggie approached the sentry box and inquired after Joe, asking the soldier if she could see him. As the soldier was making inquiries Maggie felt like running away. She was very nervous about this meeting. Was she making a mistake? Would Joe even want to see her? Her heart fell when the soldier told her Joe was in County Cork. His company had been transferred down there; Maggie was devastated Joe had not told her he was going. They both turned for home and Maggie was sobbing, Mary told her she was a fool to be crying over him. Maggie's sobbing turned to sadness then anger all at once. She felt a closeness to him that she had never felt with anyone else and she had thought he felt the same way. She turned to Mary and said, "I never want to see or talk to Joe Moran again." Before Maggie and Mary parted they made arrangements to go to dance that same evening. She would soon forget Joe Moran ever existed.

Life returned to normal for Maggie. She went to dances and parties and also dated some other local boys, although it was never serious. She thought of Joe constantly, but it was now over three months since he had left Dublin. Her brother Patsy was married and he and his wife opened a shop in Pimlico and ran a taxi business as well. Maggie and Mary went out dancing one night. As they were sitting with their friends a young man approached Maggie and asked her to dance. He was a soldier and he was stationed at Collins Barracks. A flood of memories came back to Maggie about Joe. She was trying to pluck up the courage to inquire about Joe, but the dance ended and the soldier asked Maggie if she would like a drink. She usually would not have agreed but in this case she would make an exception. They were seated and talking when Maggie broached the subject and asked him if he knew a Joe Moran who was once stationed at the Barracks. "Of course I do. I just left him at the bar in Thomas Street two hours ago." Maggie was flabbergasted. "Oh, how is he and how long has he been back in Dublin?" she asked. "He is a lot better now and on the mend," said the soldier. "What are you talking about?" she asked. "Has he been hurt?" The soldier then told her when they were on maneuvers in Cork they were scaling the side of a mountain on the seashore when Joe's rope snapped without warning and he fell fifty feet to the beach below. He suffered two broken legs and fractured his skull. He was unconscious for thirty-six hours and the doctor said his recovery was due to his very good physical condition. Maggie was crying now and the young soldier was concerned.

"What is the matter?" he asked her. Maggie told him Joe was her friend. The soldier said that Joe would probably still be in Thomas Street and if Maggie would like to see him he would take her. Maggie called Mary and told her what had happened and they all left the dance and caught a horse drawn cab to go and see Joe. When they arrived at the pub, Maggie asked them both to let her go in by herself. She entered the bar and could not see him. She asked the barman if a Joe Moran was in. He replied that he was in the snug, and would she kindly leave the bar as no women were allowed. She should have known better. She went around to the snug where four people were sitting enjoying their pints of beer. When she spotted Joe, he did not see her. She watched him from her safe position in the doorway. His face was scarred and he had lost a lot of weight. There was also a walking stick at his side. Maggie backed out of the snug and ran outside. Her sobs were uncontrollable. What happened? What had happened to her beloved Joe? The thought of Joe having suffered made Maggie's heart ache. Mary saw the agonized look on Maggie's face. "He looks so hurt and sick," Maggie said. "I can't face him. I feel so ashamed for thinking of myself and never imagining anything like that happening to Joe. I should have known there was a reason he hadn't kept in touch." Maggie and Mary took their leave of the young soldier after thanking him. On the way home Maggie was still very upset. "Mary I can't face him, and I don't think he would like me to see him in his condition." As much as Mary wanted to disagree with Maggie she held her tongue and nodded her agreement.

Joe was having some discomfort with his legs. He slowly stretched them out in the cozy snug. He was thinking of Maggie and missing her. She would never be with the likes of him. He could be an invalid for all he knew. Joe was contemplating when he had last seen Maggie. He had spent two weeks confined to Barracks when his company was suddenly sent to Cork on maneuvers. There had been no time to tell Maggie where he was, and then this accident happened. Now she would never have anything to do with him, especially in his condition.

His thoughts were interrupted when the barman came into the snug. "How are you Joe? That was a nice young lady that was asking after you." "What young lady? I didn't see anyone." "She must have left," the barman went on to explain to Joe that he had told her to leave the bar. Joe was elated. My God, he thought, it could only be Maggie. Joe made his way slowly out of the snug and looked down Thomas Street. There was no sign of her. He then made his way down Bridgefoot Street hill but still no sign.

As Maggie and Mary were crossing Queen Street Bridge, Maggie's thoughts were still on Joe. How forlorn and lonely he had looked. "Mary I'm going back to see Joe," she said. "God bless you Maggie," Mary replied. As Maggie made her way back up Bridgefoot Street Bridge she saw Joe hobbling down.

God she loved that man. As they approached each other he saw her and smiled. Maggie ran into Joe's arms and they kissed. The kiss was shaded by a desperate longing. "What sort of a man are you, not getting in touch with me?" Maggie asked.... Joe was so happy just looking at Maggie he couldn't think of anything to say." What happened to you?" she asked again. .Joe collected his thoughts and related the story.

"When I left you that night I was escorted back to Collin's Barracks. I was a week cleaning stables and general duties. I was not allowed to leave my quarters so I could not get in touch with you. One morning at around 4 a.m., we awoke to the sound of the bugle and in no time we found ourselves loaded into trucks and heading for Cork on maneuvers. We arrived late in the day in Fermoy, a small farming town where we had dinner, a few drinks and slept. The next morning I was fecking hanging off a cliff on a rope and then flying through the air. That was the last thing I remembered until I woke in the local hospital. I felt as though I was returning from a pit. I couldn't focus on anything. The doctors told me I was doing a lot of shouting and the pain was unbearable. The nurse gave me some sort of powder in water and the pain subsided. I was like this for a number of days, drifting in and out of consciousness. I am on the road to recovery but I don't know what the future holds for me as far as the army is concerned. However, I did miss you Maggie and I am sorry I couldn't get in touch with you. Maggie was smiling,

"What is it?" Joe asked.

"Well I was trying to picture you swinging off a cliff," she said.

They both started laughing.

"If only you could have seen me Maggie, I was a regular Tarzan."

Maggie asked Joe back for some tea.

"I can't," he replied. "I am still in the army and I have to be back at the Barracks in the next hour."

A look of disappointment crossed Maggie's face. "Well maybe some other time" she said and Joe knew she was disappointed.

"What about you and I go to the pictures tomorrow night?" he asked, Maggie's face lit up. "That would be lovely," she replied.

As they took leave of each other at Queen Street Bridge, they said their good-byes. Joe slowly made his way up the Quays. Back at the Barracks Joe was sitting on his bunk thinking of the wonderful meeting he had just had, then like a thunderbolt it hit him. What a fool he was, he thought. Here was this beautiful girl worried sick about him, asking him back to her home for something to eat and here he was sitting alone in the Barracks. Joe got up to leave when he was stopped at the gate.

"What's up Joe?" the sentry Paddy asked. Joe went on to explain.

"I have got to see my girl, cover up for me and I will be back shortly."

"You will get me shot," the sentry said "but go ahead and don't be long."

"Thanks Paddy," Joe replied and with that hailed a horse drawn cab and was soon outside of Maggie's house.

The house was in darkness but he had to see her and

took a chance by throwing some pebbles at the bedroom window. Maggie's brother Mick was woken out of a deep sleep with the rattling sound; he pulled the curtains aside and looked out. He saw a figure outside with what looked like a burglar's tool in his hand. He immediately woke his brother Ritchie.

"Come on he whispered someone is trying to break into the house."

"What the feck!" Ritchie shouted as he awoke with a start. Soon all the house was awake.

"What's wrong" Catherine cried.

"Someone is trying to break into the house," was the reply. "He must be crazy if he thinks there is money in this house". With that, Maggie's two brothers made their way downstairs. Ritchie went out of the back way picking up his hurling stick and Mick went out of the front. Holding a walking stick Maggie and Catherine were shaking in their bedroom. Ritchie and Mick came at Joe together, when suddenly Mick stopped. "Joe he cried what the feck are you doing?" Joe nearly fell over with fright. "What the hell!" he shouted. When Maggie heard Joe's name she ran downstairs." Joe what's the matter?" "I'm sorry I woke you all, but Maggie I have to talk to you. "It better be fecking important," Ritchie replied, "waking up all the house at this time of night." "Stop cursing," Catherine scolded. "Maggie can I talk to you alone?" asked Joe again. "No," Ritchie shouted. "Anything you have to say you can say in front of the family, no respectable girl should be alone with a man she hardly knows at this hour of the night." "Maggie, will you marry me? There is no one in this world I would rather spend my life with. I love you very much." There was complete silence and shock. No one said anything for a couple of moments. Joe felt very awkward. Maybe she doesn't love me, he thought. Maybe I am making a complete fool of myself. Suddenly he heard Maggie's voice. "Of course I will marry you, you idiot. I was expecting a more romantic setting, but I would be honoured to be your wife Joe Moran." Everyone starting laughing, Mick said to Joe "I nearly killed you. I thought that walking stick you have was a burglar's tool."

They all went back into the house and Maggie put the kettle on.
"Would you like a drink and something to eat Joe?" she asked.
"Maggie if you put a horse in front of me I will eat it." Joe realized he had not eaten all day as he had been feeling very depressed, but now what an ending to a day

that had started out miserably. Maggie and Joe were married in Arron's Quay Church. Ritchie was the best man. They rented a flat in Oliver Bond house in H Block just off Bridgefoot Street Hill.

Happy memories came flooding back to Maggie as she looked at Joe. Here she was having their ninth child and he was still the man for her. Maggie was brought back to reality when Joe said, "Maggie I am naming this baby Bernard after my grandfather."

Maggie was surprised, as he had never bothered with names before this. Bernard was a nice name.

"All right," she replied. "But Joe this is the last child."

He just smiled and said, "Sure Maggie, sure."

CHAPTER 4

When I was brought home from the hospital there was a great fuss made of me in Oliver Bond House where my family lived right in the heart of Dublin. Years ago Oliver Bond was used as housing for the army. Every entrance had gates, so when trouble started the police used to shut the gates. The people who lived in this area were the salt of the earth, but dare a stranger come in looking for trouble, they never came again. It was a very "clannish" community that way. There were only two bedrooms and a parlor, so with eleven people living in the house, life was hard. Looking back I still don't know how we managed, but somehow we did. Joey was the eldest, then Roseleen, Carmel, Paddy, Kitty, Gerry, Tony, Noel and me, Bernard. It was a very rough time and in the entire project there must have been over three hundred kids. You can imagine what life was like. My father worked for my uncle Patsy Hennesey who owned three cabs. My father Joe, whose nickname was Bugs made a living, but just about. There was never much money but we always had enough to eat. We used to play soccer in front of the flats, about fifty to a side. There were so many fights and scraps you wouldn't believe, however, we always made up. That was just the sort of rapport we had and it was always lots of fun.

On one occasion when I was about 10 years of age, I climbed a gate and as I was sitting on top of it a hand grabbed me by the hair. It was Bang-Bang and he let me go and I ran away, but was I ever scared. Bang-Bang was everywhere in Dublin. He used to jump from bus to bus with a large house key in his hand shooting everyone and calling out Bang-Bang - hence his nickname. The kids in Dublin loved him. He was harmless and there was always great excitement whenever he appeared. Another time my sister Carmel and her friend Maureen Scully were looking after me. We were all standing at the entrance to Oliver Bond when the district nurse came by. "Who is that lovely boy?" she asked. I replied "feck off." I don't remember but my sister never stopped relating the story over the years - nice boy hey?

My brothers all went to Brunswick Street School, except my brother Noel and I who went to John's Lane School, situated on the corner of Thomas Street. My mother used to be up every morning at 6 a.m. making breakfast and packing lunches. We used to eat in order of our ages, with the oldest sitting down for meals first. My grandmother Catherine came to live with us as she was unable to cope on her own and we were delighted to have her. She was forever looking for her purse. She would hide it in the most unexpected places and when she couldn't find it she told our neighbours we stole her money. She was a grand old lady. Every Sunday morning we all had to line up before her and then she would dole out one penny to each of us. On our way to mass we would buy a stick of rock (a hard sweet). My grandmother would look after us when my mother went to work. She used to try putting us to bed at 5 p.m. and on one occasion I was playing soccer with my friends when she came down the stairs and called for me to come up. She was calling, "Please son come into the house" when much to my shame I told her to "feck off" and ran off leaving her calling after me. On many occasions she would burn the food and wandered around the house during the night. She would ask my mother "who is that man sitting at the fire." It was my father. We all used to think it was very funny but of course we did not know she had dementia - God love her. All the houses in Dublin had fireplaces in which we burned turf. It came from the bogs in the country part of Ireland and was very clean and economical. We were in bed one night when we heard a terrific crash. We all ran to investigate and found my grandmother had collapsed and fallen with the side of her face into the fire. We rushed her to St. Kevin's Hospital in my father's taxi. Her face was terribly blistered and burned quite badly but she didn't feel the pain as her nerve endings where damaged. When she was discharged from the hospital two months later, grandmother knew no one. It was very sad to watch her just sitting there. Mom did everything for her but to no avail. My beloved grandmother died at 4 a.m. January 1953. She was 93 years of age, God bless her. Her funeral was one of the largest Dublin had seen. All of the people from the Liberties attended, including all of her old neighbors from Bow Street and Queen Street. It was a great send off. At least she would be with the only man she knew, her husband Paddy Hennessey. May they both be in God's hands.

Soon after this my beautiful sister Kitty died of pneumonia. My mother and father were devastated. I don't think my father was ever the same again, as he was besotted with Kitty. The house in Oliver Bond was never the same again either. There were just too many unhappy memories. My mother went to the corporation housing authority and asked for another house. When she explained the reasons they gave us a house in Inchicore about four miles from the city. It may as well have been 100 miles as it was a real country place to us.

My first impression of Inchicore was one of awe. There was a canal behind our house where we could swim. There were lots of fields surrounding us and we had a big back and front garden, as well as a soccer field and dirt paths where we could ride bikes. It was a paradise for my brothers and me. It was very strange to us as we were city kids, but there were also lots of kids our own ages. Life settled down for the Moran family after our losses. We even acquired a dog that we called Darkie, a beautiful Kerry Blue. Some of my brothers were working by this time and some of them still traveled to Brunswick Street School. My youngest brother and I still went to John's Lane School every morning. My mother used to give me four pennies for bus fare for Noel and I. I used to make him walk with me to town, then leave him at the school gate and pretend I was going into school. Then I'd I take off. I played truant and used to spend my day walking around the fruit market on Green Street. When I felt hungry I would steal some fruit and also help the vendors set up their stalls and lift boxes. In return they gave me a penny. With that and the bus fare I had saved I bought some loose cigarettes called Woodbines and they were very strong.

I remember the first time I inhaled my Woodbine it made me so dizzy, but still I smoked it. When it was time to pick up Noel I would make my way to an alley called the Forty Steps. There was a lot of loose ground and I had a hiding spot where I would stash my treasure (Woodbines and school satchel). I would then carry on, picking up Noel on the way and we would go down to a government centre called the Bano, where they used to give us a bun and a cup of cocoa. We would play for about an hour and then make our way home to Inchicore. It was a great life.

When any of us had problems with our teeth, our mother would take us to a dental training hospital where dental students checked them free of charge. There was another place she took us for medical checkups, free of course and they used to give us a spoon of cod liver oil. What a terrible taste. My Mom knew how to stretch a shilling, she had to with our gang. Life for us during this period was great. One day I was swimming with my brothers in the canal when I met my life-long friends, Johnny Anders and Noel Flanagan. It didn't go so well at first. I was swimming when I felt a big splash beside me. It was Johnny and Noel throwing branches into the canal. "Feck off," I shouted. One word led to another with Johnny who challenged me to a fight. He was about my age, but where I was slim, he was well built. Still, we were fearless. I jumped out of the water butting him in the face, trying to do the most damage first as indicative of my Oliver Bond upbringing. To this day I think it was the toughest fight I had. We expended lots of energy, but no one won. We ended up on the ground each holding the other in a headlock, saying "you let go and then I will." We must have been like this for half an hour when my brothers came along and split us up. I did not see Johnny and Noel until a week later. They were playing soccer and I was just standing there watching when Noel, whom we called Eggo because he was very tall and skinny, asked if I wanted to play, thereafter, the three of us where inseparable. In fact, we decided to form a soccer team. Mr. Finnigan from our street, Jamestown Ave., decided to be our manager/coach. We had no soccer uniforms and to raise money collected old newspapers and clothing. In no time we had enough to purchase striped jerseys and shorts. We signed up in the local league that was composed of Bluebell, Ballyfermet, Drimnagh and Kilmainham. They are all the districts in and around Inchicore. We called ourselves the Jamestown Rangers. New friends were made and we soon had a local following. Our first game was against Bluebell and we easily won. There were at least two games a week. Johnny, Eggo and I were the defense. We lost some and won some until eventually we were in the semi finals against Kilmainham. We were winning 1-0 by half time and were pretty cocky. In the second half Kilmainham scored two goals in five minutes. Mr. Finnigan really lost his temper and it was enough to pull us all together and we won 3-2. Here we were in our first season and we had made it to the finals. We had to face Drimnagh next. They had the most established team in the district. Their top players were Eddy Hickey and Liam Lynam. We started to train in earnest. Every spare moment we were in the fields practicing, until eventually the big day arrived. We were to play in Bluebell which that was neutral ground. It was a perfect day for soccer, sunny and cold. Drimnagh won the toss and the game started. We were five minutes into play when a Drimnagh player was warned about tripping. By the end of the first half the referee was furious, and as the game progressed it just got dirtier. When the whistle sounded for the end of the first half the score was 0-0. This game was turning into something we never expected. We realized we had a chance as we figured that Drimnagh would be ahead by this time. Their two great players were playing really hard, but Eggo was marking Liam and keeping him in check.

This whistle sounded for the second half. We bounced out of our seats all ready to go. We were ten minutes into the game when there was a commotion on the field. Eggo and Liam were rolling on the ground punching each other, when they were finally separated they were both expelled from the game. We settled down again when I kicked the ball and the sole on my boot came loose. All I could hear was my boot flapping. It was a mediocre second half with little was happening and the score was still 0-0. I was in left field daydreaming, when all of a sudden the ball landed in front of me. I was more than halfway down the field when to this day I still don't know how I did it. I kicked the ball with my floppy boot and it went like a rocket spinning right into the goal. There was complete silence. Everybody, including myself, was amazed. Then pandemonium broke, and there was such a cheer. It was my proudest moment. We had won the finals 1-0. I was a hero for a day. We played soccer for a few more seasons until it phased out. Jamestown Avenue was a small road but there were plenty of kids. We spent most of our leisure hours hanging around the street comer playing poker and showing off in front of the local girls. The girls taught us how to jive. Some nights we would be preoccupied talking and joking with the girls when suddenly the older blokes would creep up on us and if we had cigarettes take them off us. If we saw them approaching we would scatter in all directions because if they caught us they would make us sing at the top of our voices. This would of course bring out the neighbours who shouted at us to be quiet.

Another thing they would do is to take our pants off and hang them on a lamppost. It
was all in fun but we would be thoroughly embarrassed. The girls would be in hysterics laughing at us. Eggo was the funniest as he used to go crazy if he was caught. He was really quite shy. When we played cards with had our few pennies on the ground they would take them from us and tell us to get home or threaten to call the police and tell them we were gambling. One night we were all in Dan Wall's playing snooker. The girls were having an ice cream in the cafe next door to the snooker tables and we were showing off how tough we were when our crowd came in. "What the feck are you blokes doing out at this hour of the night?" It was 10 p.m. and Christy Doyle lined us

up against the wall and started to lecture us about the error of our ways like a priest. He was very funny. He went on about us playing snooker, smoking and being with the girls. He said they would have to teach us hooligans a lesson and with that they tied us up, gagged us and left us tied to the chairs while they took the girls home. We were there for hours and when the owner, Dan Wall came in, he pretended he didn't notice us and proceeded to lock up. We were fecking frantic, the lights were turned off and then silence. Johnny was the first to get his gag off. "What the Feck is happening?" he cried. There was some scurrying on the floor and Johnny said, "I think there are rats in here." We were in pitch blackness. There was such a clatter of chairs, the noise of everyone moving around was deafening. Of course the lights were thrown on and Dan and our blokes would come in laughing their heads off— very jolly!

We used to go to Drogheda, which was approximately 30 or 40 miles from Dublin. We would make sure the big blokes never knew were we were going but somehow they always found out. Again they would find our campsite and when we were sleeping they would chain all our bikes together. Of course when we woke up we didn't know what had happened and would sit for hours trying to break the chains. Then they'd they appear laughing their heads off again. It was all in fun and we loved them. On one occasion a crowd of us were walking up Manor Street in Dublin when we heard a big commotion. It was Bang-Bang shooting everyone with his large key. He didn't talk, he shouted. He was quite small with jet black hair and the largest eyes. When he spotted us he shouted, "I am deputizing all of you as posse, there are bad people about. We used to get a great a kick out of him and one of the lads said, "Where are our badges?" "No badges," he shouted. "You don't need them." With that we all followed him down to Benburb Street with Bang-Bang shouting at everyone along the way. God he was a lovable character. When we reached Arron Quay he told us all the bad people had gone and he wanted his badges back. When we reminded him that he did not give us any badges he just smiled and ran off. We where all laughing thinking about him just kidding us, when all of a sudden he came up behind us and shouted, "Where are my fecking badges?" making us jump out of our skins. Then he was gone in a flash down an alley laughing his head off. What a bloke.

Johnny Forty Coats used to hang out at the fruit market.

How he survived I will never know. I didn't know the history of these lovable characters but I do remember one incident. I was walking down Green Street on a bitterly cold day when I spotted Johnny Forty Coats. He was standing in a doorway looking very forlorn and I did feel sorry for him. I had a few shillings in my pocket and approached him and offered it to him. He just stared at me. Again I tried to offer him the money, but he replied in the most gentlest of voices, "Please give it to someone who needs it." I was taken aback. Here was this poor soul, cold, hungry, with nowhere to sleep, telling me to give my money to someone who needs it. I looked into his soft eyes and serene face and even at my young age I knew he was one of the most exceptional people I was ever likely to meet. I will never forget that face, or his most humble demeanor. God bless him.

Our local cinema was called the Core and for Sunday night movies you had to book in advance. At Saturday night dances we all made sure we had a date because everyone in our group used to have dates for the Sunday night show. I needn't tell you it was hilarious, the remarks that were made by our crowd to each other. If you tried to put your arm around a girl, Christy Doyle would immediately say "We will have none of that." You always had to be on your best behaviour. One Sunday night as we all were watching the Story of Bernadette when Eggo went down to the foyer for some ice cream for himself and his girlfriend. When he returned to his seat everything was silent and as he made his way down the aisle his seat, he genuflected, made the sign of the cross and sat down. Well the whole balcony broke into uncontrollable laughter at

Eggo who had been daydreaming and thought he was in church. I had never seen Eggo so embarrassed. He bent down to his girlfriend and the two of them just stood up and walked out, followed by Johnny, myself and our dates close behind.

Razor Throat's nickname came from the fact that he was never shaved and always looked as though he was between a beard and a week's growth. He was small with shoulder-length hair and wore a long overcoat which he tucked around his throat and grasped with his hand. His hangout was around Christchurch where there was a small park with benches where he used to sleep and collect the odd shilling or two from the people who passed by. There was also a soup kitchen on Island Street that would feed the down and outs and there was always a crowd there. Dublin was a city with a high unemployment rate at the time. One day as I was passing the soup kitchen there was a commotion. I went over to see what was happening. They nearly always served broth to the street people and on this occasion they were serving clear soup. This was not going down well with Razor Throat who was insisting on his broth. Some people in the crowd were having fun and egging Razor on. He was saying if that if he was not served broth he would take his business elsewhere. He was causing such a fuss that the Brother who was in charge came out to see what was happening. When he heard the story, he apologized and handed Razor a shilling to go the restaurant across the Quays where he could get some broth. A big cheer abounded with Razor proudly walking away saying, "I'll eat here again."

CHAPTER 5

There was a boy's club in Inchicore named St. Joseph's; it had a new boxing club so we all decided to join. Thinking back, some of my happiest times were spent at St. Joseph's. We used to play table tennis, push-penny and go on outings. The parish priest in the Oblates was Father Divine, who we called Pop Divine, and he used to oversee the everyday running of the club. He had a stutter and every kid in Inchicore loved him.

Pop Divine ran the parish very strictly, and when we were in church he had no qualms about reading your name from the pulpit. We used to stand at the back of the church and Christy Boyle who used to make funny noises. Eggo could not control himself and always burst out laughing. Pop Divine would stop the sermon and say, "Hello Mr. Flanagan, would you like to share the joke with everyone?" Eggo was one of the shyest people I know and this would make us all lose it. In the meantime Eggo would have a face like a beetroot. Pop would tell us to leave and come back when we could behave ourselves. Of course we would be on our knees with laughter outside the church.

Christy, who had started all of this, would remain in church with his face never changing. You would think he was a saint. He did the same every Sunday morning. When we went to St. Joseph's club Pop would come over from the church and reprimand us for our bad behavior. We would be sorry and tell him we would not disrupt mass again. Alas, it was not to be for Christy would be at his antics again and again. No matter where we sat, it was enough to look in his direction to start us off again. Mr. O'Hara was the boxing coach for the club and a school teacher at the Oblates school. He was a robust man from County Kerry. He put us through various training programs and we loved it. Our club was picked to fight another club in Dublin City called the Newspaper Boys Boxing Club. Its reputation preceded it as it was an old and established club with a winning record. There were to be seven fights in the Stadium Boxing Club. Eggo, Johnny and I were picked to fight. As the big day approached we were very excited. We traveled by coach to the stadium and felt very important. Our best boxer was Brendan Lard and Mr. O'Hara decided he would fight first. It gave us confidence, as there were to be only three round fights.

When the bell went for the first round, Brendan came out of his corner and the other kid didn't know what hit him. Brendan won easily in the first round. Our next fight was a kid named Archie McGurk. He was a big lump of a fellow, and he did not fair well. The Newspaper Club kid was using him as a punching bag. In the third round an extraordinary thing happened. As Archie was being bashed he suddenly butted and kneed his opponent. He was immediately disqualified. Eggo was up next. His opponent came into the ring, a well-built kid with massive shoulders and a hairy chest. Eggo was very skinny and tall, but their weight corresponded. When Eggo saw his opponent he panicked saying, "Who the feck is he? I'm not fighting him." He turned to me and said "Bernard will you fight him?" "Feck off' I replied. Johnny and I could not control our laughter as it was the most misplaced pair of fighters we had ever seen.

The bell went for the first round and Eggo had to be pushed from his corner. His opponent came at him with a flurry of punches. "What the hell!" Eggo shouted. It was the funniest round we had ever seen. Eggo was running from one corner to another with his opponent throwing punches from all directions. You could hear the wind every time he threw a punch. Eggo kept grabbing him, and every time the referee broke them up then turned away, Eggo punched his opponent making Hairy Chest furious. Johnny and I were uncontrollable with laughter, showing no concern for Eggo. The first round was over and Eggo's body was red with punches. Mr. O'Hara stopped the fight and was furious with the other coach for putting this experienced boxer against Eggo. He was trying to get the fight disqualified. The referee eventually agreed and a delighted Eggo vowed he would never step into the ring again.

Eggo turned to Johnny and myself saying, "Thanks for the support you two." We were still laughing. It was my turn to fight next. I won the fight on points, as did Johnny. Herbie Flanders from our club was the next one to fight. He also won and our club won the tournament. It was a very enjoyable and funny experience to be remembered with nostalgia for years to come.

My brother Noel and I were still going to John's Lane School, and still walking and saving the bus fare to buy cigarettes. I was still skipping school and played truant for about two years without getting caught. One day as my older brothers were coming home from Brunswick Street School Tony was walking on the wall of the river Liffey when he fell in. My other brother Gerry jumped in to pull him out, but both of them were in trouble struggling in the water. My brother Paddy whose arm was in a cast also jumped in to try to help but soon realized he too was in trouble. They were being pulled by the tide down past Queen Street Bridge. There was a lot of commotion and a man with a baker's van stopped to see what was going on. When he realized what was happening, he jumped in without hesitation and grabbed them one at a time pulling them over to a ladder on the side of the wall and swimming back for the next. Thankfully he was able to rescue the three of them. The headlines in the paper the next day read: "Three boys rescued by baker. That was how my brothers and I were, if one was in trouble, no matter what the danger, we didn't hesitate to help.

Another day when Noel and I arrived home from school we found our mother crying. Our eldest brother Joey had run away to Belfast and joined the Royal Air Force. We really missed him. He was to remain in the air force for more than twenty years. Soon after this Noel and I transferred to the Oblate Fathers School in Inchicore, which I thoroughly enjoyed. My teacher was Mr. O'Hara, our coach from boxing. I had one bad experience. One day I was daydreaming in class and Mr. O'Hara smacked me across the head. I immediately retaliated without thinking and jumped out of my seat and butted him right on the face. I don't know who was more surprised, him or me. There was blood trickling from his nose. He sent me home and told me to report the next day to Pop Divine at the church. When I went to see him the next day I was shaking. I entered his office and he glared at me. "What am I going to do with you?" he asked. "I think I will have to expel you." Here I was just three months into my new school and I was to be expelled. My mother would kill me. "Do you go to mass and solidarity regularly?" he asked. "I do," I replied. He carried on questioning me for about an hour. I thought the interview would never end. "I will let you stay in school, but if anything like this ever happens again I will expel you." He said I was to report back to the headmaster and also apologize to Mr. O'Hara and my class. "Now leave," he said. I was never so glad to get out of that office. I was still shaking. As I passed his outside window I could see him smiling. I returned to school and went straight to the headmaster's office. Mr. Boyle was a small, stocky individual. I had seen him walking around the school yard but I had never talked to him. "So you are the boy that struck Mr. O'Hara?" he asked. "Yes sir," I replied. "What have you got to say for yourself?" "I'm sorry." He went on to say that they would not tolerate this sort of behavior. He told me to put out my hand. It was the first time I had ever felt the leather strap. He gave me twenty lashes across my hands, ten on each, and it was a very painful experience. When he was finished he sent me back to class. I pretended it had not hurt but, in fact, it was terrible. Mr. O'Hara was standing at the blackboard. "Well young man, what do have to say for you?" I apologized to the class for my behavior and then Mr. O'Hara told me to put out my hands. I don't think he realized that I had already been punished by Mr. Boyle and continued to give me the same punishment I had just received. Again I pretended it did not hurt and did not flinch, but my fingers were very swollen. When he had finished he told me to sit down and that would be the end of it. When I returned home from school I was in a lot of pain. When my father saw my hands he went wild. I tried to stop him from going to see Mr. O'Hara as he was a boxer and I did not want my father to get hurt. The lads at school told me later that my father had just walked into the classroom where Mr. O'Hara was cleaning up and my teacher did not stand a chance. My father knocked him all over the classroom. It's strange, all boys think of their fathers as old, but Bugs still had it. I was proud of him at that moment. When I returned to school nothing more was ever said about this incident. One thing I would have to say about O'Hara, he was not vengeful and he treated me fairly from then on. Life settled back to normal. They used to show movies in St. Joseph's club. Johnny, Eggo and I spent most of our time at the club and it was terrific. The people in charge were the Brothers from the Oblate Fathers. They decided to take the club members for a weeks outing. The excitement this caused was tremendous. I don't think any one of us had even been outside of Dublin. We were going to stay in a castle in County Offaly. About fifty of us were going and our chaperones were Brothers Lacy and Maher and Pop Devine. The cost was 7 shillings and 6 pence which was quite a lot of money at the time, but somehow my father came up with it. We were leaving for the trip on Friday and it was now Monday. I couldn't sleep with the excitement. Eventually Friday arrived and the coach picked us up at the Oblates School. When we arrived at the castle in Offaly we couldn't believe the scenery. It was one of the most beautiful of counties, with green fields and rivers. In fact, it was a school boy's dream. The castle itself was incredible, with long corridors, lots of spiral stairs and secret passages. We played 'hide and seek' and a game called 'relievio.' It consisted of picking pick teams and having one side hide while the other tried to find you. They would mark a square as they caught you, and then you had to stand in this square. When everyone in the team was caught it was the turn of the other team to hide. You could also free your group if you were able to sneak up on the square without being seen and run through the square shouting "relievio" (this was really maddening for the opposing team). The castle was so vast with so many rooms and hiding spots that no one could find anyone. One night after supper it was getting dark and we were all in the woods playing when all of a sudden Eggo came screaming up to us and shouted, "There's a ghost in the woods." We were all laughing when suddenly two figures in white came towards us from a clump of trees. Well, the commotion this caused was incredible, and we all ran for our lives.

Eggo was in front and as we caught up to him we pulled him back as not one of us wanted to be last, his screams were unbelievable. We made it back to the castle where Pop Devine asked us what the matter was. We related the story and he seemed genuinely shocked. We were all getting ready for bed when one of the boys asked Pop if we could go out to see if we could find our ghosts. He agreed, so back to the woods we went with our flashlights. Once again we saw the two figures approaching the castle and once again we all scattered back to where Pop Devine was standing by the gate with a stick in his hand summoning us to get back to bed at once. We had all been in bed about five minutes when Pop Devine and the brothers came in shining flashlights in our faces saying if anyone was still awake there would be trouble. Of course we all pretended to be asleep. Later on we found out that it had been an elaborate plan by Pop Devine. The ghosts had been brothers Lacy and Maher with sheets covering them. Another incident occurred during our time in County Offlay when Johnny and I visited the local sweet shop. We were returning to the castle when this little person in a long black coat tried to talk to us. He made an attempt to open the fly on my pants. We used to call these men 'fancy boys.' We were pretty innocent and did not know much about this sort of behavior. Johnny and I both bolted across the fields as he ran after us. Suddenly Johnny said, "Hey Bernard let's get this bloke." We turned back and ran at him. He stopped in complete surprise. I jumped on him and hit him in the face and Johnny hit him in the stomach. He started to run and we kicked him on the arse. Hopefully he wouldn't bother any more kids. Unfortunately, our fantastic holiday had to come to an end and we returned to Dublin. It had to be one of the most terrific times we had ever spent. When I returned back home everyone seemed sad. I asked what was the matter and my Mam told me my Dad had had an accident. He was at the Phoenix Park horse races in one of the paddocks when suddenly a race horse had panicked and kicked my Dad in the face knocking him unconscious. He was in hospital but his injuries were not that serious— a broken nose and some stitches in his cheek. When he returned home he looked very tough with a long white scar down his face. He was awarded 400 pounds for this accident— that was a fortune in those days— and it certainly made life a little easier for a while.

CHAPTER 6

I have a date to go to the pictures," said Eggo. Johnny and I were caught by surprise as Eggo did not make many dates. "Tell us more," Johnny urged. We were both looking at Eggo with newfound respect. "Her name is Beth Convey from Kilmainham and I met her through my sister." Kilmainham was about a mile from our district. "Then she hasn't met you yet?" I asked "Did your sister make the date for you?" Eggo was the shyest person I knew, and I was teasing him. "Feck off," he said. "I asked her myself and she could not say yes quickly enough. You blokes don't know how charming I can be when the need arises and if you don't be quiet I won't tell you the next news." Seemingly Eggo's sister had these friends in Kilmainham and when they were visiting Eggo's house this one girl Beth Convey who had always liked Eggo asked Eggo's sister to fix her up on a date. Eggo agreed if her friends would date Johnny and me. We were flabbergasted. However, we all would be going to the Inchicore Cinema. We were excited but where would we get the money from? We needed 36 pence each, and when we needed money we usually collected scrap copper, I'm ashamed to say, from any source. If we had scrap wire we used to burn off the plastic and underneath was shiny new wiring. When we had accumulated about 10lbs of it we sold it to a scrap metal dealer in Island Bridge. We also had to be careful as the Garda paid regular visits to this particular scrap yard. There was a factory at the top of Jamestown Road that always had copper and brass at the back. We decided to break in the next night by climbing over a high gate. It was a pitch black night, drizzling with rain and cold when we finally made it over the gate. We were in an awful state, wet and dirty, but there was a bonanza of scrap there. We proceeded to throw it over the gate and then went back for more. We were making a terrible noise, as professionals we were not. I don't know how we weren't caught as there were quite a few houses around. When we finally had enough scrap we climbed back over the gate and started to put our loot into old sacks. We carried what we could a couple of hundred yards further into the fields where were we had a pre-arranged hiding place and covered it over with leaves and branches, then rushed home.

The next day we went to check on our ill-gotten gains and found we had some pretty good stuff, brass ingots and plates and lots of copper wire. We loaded up a pull cart that we had brought with us and started off for the scrap dealers. We were shaking when we arrived and asked for the dealer.

"We have some old copper for sale," we said. "Will you

buy it?"

We were trying to be so cool, and he told us to throw it on the scales and then asked us were we had gotten it from. We told him we had picked it up at the dump. He just smiled and handed us three pound notes. We could not get out fast enough and once outside we split the money and were delighted with ourselves. We now had enough for our dates.

Sunday soon arrived and we went to pick up the girls. We had previously arranged to meet them outside St. Michael's Chapel in Inchicore and were full of nerves and bravado. The three girls were waiting outside the church and they all looked really pretty. We were now extremely nervous and Eggo said, "Hello, sorry we are late." The look on their faces when they saw Johnny and me made me think they weren't very impressed with us, which did little for our confidence.

"I'm Bernard and this is Johnny," I said. I really didn't know what I was saying, however, they smiled and linked our arms as we made our way to the cinema. We were a bit early for the movie to start and so we went for an ice cream at Dan Walls, our local snooker hall and restaurant. Just as we were about to sit down Beth smacked Eggo gently across the face. Johnny and I started laughing when Johnny's date told us if a girl smacks a boy on the face she likes him. I forgot to mention that Johnny's date was about a foot taller than him and they looked quite funny walking together. Eggo and I did not dare to say anything and just smiled at them. When we started to leave for the movies, Johnny who was standing near me whispered, "I would not like to see her Mom and Dad—they must be fecking giants."

When we entered the movies a lot of our group was

already there with their girlfriends. Of course we had to run the gauntlet. They were making kissing sounds and saying did our Mammies let us out and when did we start wearing long pants. We did not know where to put our faces but it all stopped when the movie finally started, it was a cowboy film.

We all sat in different rows and about halfway into the movie we heard someone being smacked hard on the face. It was Eggo. Johnny leaned over to my seat and whispered to me, "She must fecking really love him." Of course I really lost it and could not stop laughing. The usher came down to our row and told me to be quiet. Of course that made it worse and I couldn't stop so he removed me from the cinema for creating a disturbance. Johnny, Eggo and the girls soon followed. We were walking the girl's home down by the canal and stopped by some waste ground to kiss the girls goodnight. Johnny was having a problem with his girlfriend because she was so tall. He got a couple of house bricks which were lying around to stand on to kiss her and once again I started laughing. The girls left and told us they would never date us again as we were all idiots. Eggo replied, "It takes one to know one." Never bandy words with us.

"We still had a lot of copper and brass hidden so a couple of days later we decided to sell some more and have a pint in a local pub called Wards in Inchicore. We were under age but that did not deter us. We all marched in very grown up like and Eggo asked for three pints. To our surprise we were served. We finished them in record time and I went up for three more. We did not finish these as quickly as we were feeling a bit groggy. It was then Johnny's turn and he asked me what I would like. I asked for an ale and raspberry. When we had finished these Johnny said he was going home as he didn't feel very well. Eggo and I went for a walk down to Tyrconnell Park to try and sober up. When we arrived there I was violently sick. It had started to snow and I was lying on the ground throwing up. Good old faithful Eggo sat down beside me and waited until I was feeling better. I said never again.

The next day we went up to our hiding place to pick up the rest of our copper and brass but discovered that most of it was gone. We found out later that my brothers had followed us and saw where we had stashed it and then helped themselves.

What was left we took down to the yard to sell. I went in by myself but didn't know that the Garda was watching and they caught me. They wanted to know who had been with me but I said I was alone and they charged me for the lot.

When my father found out he was really mad. My younger brother had also been caught playing truant and that meant the two of us had to go before the judge. I thought for sure I would be sent to Artane, which was a juvenile prison. When it was time for us to appear before the judge my mother made sure we both looked our best. My father was going with us and we all caught the bus into town. We went upstairs on the bus where my father met a friend of his. He asked my father what was going on and why were we all dressed up. My father said, "On my right I have a mitcher (truant) and on my left I have a fecking robber and we are all going to court." Noel and I started to laugh as we thought this was funny.

When it was my turn to appear before the judge he gave

me a stern lecture regarding stealing other people's property and the more he talked the more I was convinced I was going away for at least a year. Thank goodness I was only fined 10 shilling and that abruptly ended my life of crime.

CHAPTER 7

My brother Paddy was the eldest brother at home now with Joe in the Royal Air Force. I idolized Paddy. He was one of the toughest blokes in Dublin, and to me he could do anything. He was built like my father and when we were swimming he used to do the most terrific dives off the Liffey Bridge. He was the wild one of the family. Anytime I had a problem I would go to Paddy. He got me out of a lot of scrapes. He worked in Jacob's Biscuit Factory like the rest of my family. The owners were Quakers and treated all of their workers very well, even providing a recreation club where dances used to be held. They also had a running team on which Paddy used to race against other clubs, winning most of the events. He was very fit. During this time a new family moved to our avenue. Their name was Murphy, and one of the sons was called Georgie. He was a big fellow about Paddy's age. From the start he did not get on with our group and there was a lot of animosity between Georgie and a bloke called Bud Collins. Bud was a really good bloke but also a real troublemaker. Every time he was in trouble he came to our house for Paddy to help him. He listened to no one but Paddy. Bud had moved from Fatima mansions that were near Oliver Bond house in the Liberties, which was another rough and tough area of Dublin. He was not really one of our crowd but he was from our area. Georgie and Bud always clashed, with Bud always coming off worse. When Bud came to Paddy for help Paddy was reluctant to become involved because Georgie never did harm to our group. Whenever he used to pass by our corner the blokes would make remarks. To Georgie's credit, he was never scared or at least let on that he was.

Bud belonged to a large family. His father had died and

money was very short. Houses were being broken into, even a policeman's house on Jamestown Road. Our house was one of the only ones not broken into and suspicion was that one of the Morans was doing the break-ins. These robberies continued until Georgie Murphy's house was robbed and all hell broke loose. He was furious but only had a suspicion of who had done it. I met Bud one evening on the third lock bridge. He looked very smart in a new suit. The fashion in the sixties was similar to the Edwardians; (Teddy Boy) the suit coat had to be the length of your arms with a velvet collar. The pants were called drainpipes because they were so narrow (14 inches round). This was topped off with a frilly shirt and your shoes were called wedgies because they had a thick sole. Bud and I started to talk and he asked what was I up to. "Just hanging around," I replied. He asked did I want to play some snooker.

"Sure," I said but I was broke." No problem," he said as he pulled out a wad of notes from his pocket. We made our way down Inchicore Road to Dan Walls, our local snooker hall. As we passed the cinema these two blokes approached us and pushed Bud." What's going on?" I said. The tallest of the duo told me to shut up and keep out of it. Bud had had a confrontation with this fellow the week before and he was looking to beat up Bud and a few of his friends from Fatima Mansions. Suddenly without warning Bud took out a pen knife from his pocket and stabbed this bloke in the side of his head. He kept stabbing him in the arms and shoulders. The bloke didn't stand a chance. I was standing there with all sorts of thoughts going through my head. I would end up in prison as an accessory to murder, as the bloke started to fall Bud ran out and up Inchicore Road with me passing him a few seconds later. We made our way to a place called the Goat Fields where our crowd was playing soccer. Everyone was there, including Paddy. When Bud related what had happened to Paddy and the friends, everyone was in a state of shock. All of a sudden Paddy pummeled Bud." You little shit," he said. "What have you done?" Paddy was frightened because I was involved. Bud was lying on the ground crying as he had realized what he had done. Paddy shouted at me to get home and say nothing. I was home worried out of my mind. I tossed and turned all night and did not sleep a wink thinking about the poor bloke who had been stabbed. The next day I went swimming in up the canal with Johnny and Eggo. I was telling them what had happened. They too were shocked. This was not our style to use knives. A good fist fight is all that we had ever had. On the canal there are steep banks. It was a little away from the footpath. There was a crowd of blokes walking past where were we where swimming. I looked up and low and behold one of the crowd was the bloke that Bud had stabbed. Relief flooded through me as I had thought he was very badly injured or dead. He had a dressing on the side of his head and he looked okay. I dove underwater until they had passed as I did not want to be recognized. Then we all dressed hurriedly and ran back to our neighbourhood where I told the rest of our crowd the good news and everyone was relieved. Johnny's brother, Jimmy Anders, came running from the fields sweating." There's a gang from Drimnagh looking for the bloke that stabbed one of their crowd," he said. We did not want any trouble with this group as we had a good rapport with them. Sure, there was the odd fight but most of our crowd knew them and on occasions we had helped each other get out of some scrapes. As we were talking, about fifteen blokes from the Drimnagh crowd approached us. They wanted Bud. Paddy said, "He is not here and we don't want any trouble." Their leader was a massive fellow named Joxer Doyle. He was in the army and he was in no mood for excuses. Paddy said," Just go home before this gets out of hand." Joxer made a run at Paddy when his mate Benny McDonald threw a bike in front of Joxer. He fell forward and when Paddy's fist connected with his jaw, (you cold hear the punch connecting,) Joxer was knocked out cold. The Drimnagh crowd made a feeble protest but by now they were greatly outnumbered. Paddy told them to take Joxer, who was now on his feet, home. They all left muttering under their breaths. Everything settled down for a while after this. There was no sign of Bud. I think he was staying with some friends in Fatima Mansions. A week or so after this incident, my brother Gerry came home covered in blood. The Drimnagh crowd had cornered him at our local dance hall and beat up him along with Larry Byrne. My mother and father were distraught when they saw Gerry and took him to the local hospital where they took care of him. He was mostly bruised and it had looked a lot worse than it was. In the meantime Paddy had heard what had happened and was furious. The next day he and the rest of my brothers went over to Drimnagh to find the people responsible for beating up Gerry. There was no sign of them. We went looking every day for approximately two weeks with no luck. It was sometime later when were all on the Inchicore Bridge, our usual hangout, that Larry Byrne the fellow who was with Gerry when he was beaten came running over. He had spotted the gang walking up the road. There were seven of them, some of whom were from the same group we had had a run in with Bud Collins.

As they were crossing the bridge we came up behind and in front of them. They were shocked." What's the matter?" one of them shouted. "We have no trouble with you blokes." We lined them up. Paddy asked Gerry if these were the blokes responsible. Gerry is not one to become excited. He just eyed them up and down and said, "No none of these." They all relaxed. With that Gerry punched this one bloke and said this is one of them. With that we gave the seven of them a bashing. After this we didn't have any more trouble with the crowd from Drimnagh. In fact, most of them started to hang around with us the way it should be. A little time later Bud came on the scene again. He had had another run-in with Georgie. I think he was Georgie's punching bag. Of course he came to Paddy for help again. Paddy grabbed Bud by the throat and said, "You behave yourself. We will help you this time but no more knives." Word was out to deal with Georgie but it proved easier said than done. As I said before, Georgie was a big, tough bloke and when two of our group confronted him one night he beat them up. We went after him in earnest. We stopped him one night but again he fought his way out, using a horseshoe wrapped around his hand. You had to admire him. This went on for some time before we did catch him and gave him a few punches. I don't think anyone's heart was in it. We really all admired Georgie, but as usually happens one incident lead to another. Seemingly Georgie was at a dance in the Four Provinces dance hall when he was accosted by Bud and a gang from Fatima Mansions. They beat him badly. This was just not done. Bud was in trouble with us, but you never get outsiders to beat one of your neighbors. Bud did not show his face for a week or so and when we caught up with him it was me who fought him. He was older than me and we sounded off on Jamestown Avenue. Bud used to choke people until they nearly passed out. As we were fighting I was getting the better of him as I had a long reach. I cut his lip and he was also bleeding from the corner of his eye when suddenly he got me in a headlock and started to choke me. I was in trouble. While Bud was small he was very strong. As he was choking me, Johnny jumped in and pulled Bud off me. Now I was really mad. I gave Bud a severe beating. A number of the mothers on the avenue ran out and broke up the fight with Bud shouting after me that I would be sorry. From then on there were a lot of bad feelings about this incidence with repercussions lasting for years afterwards, even bringing our quarrel to England in later years.

CHAPTER 8

Johnny, Eggo and I were all the same age group from our Avenue. We were about two years younger than the main group that was approximately twenty families on our Patch. The average family had about eight children so you can imagine there were a large number of boys in our group. We came from every nook and cranny of Dublin and it made for a very interesting life style. As I look back we were all very close and when one of us was in trouble it meant you could always depend on getting help. Just around the corner from where we lived was Nash Street and Railway Avenue, a different group of people. They were a very tough crowd and we didn't bother each other. We used to bump into them occasionally at the local dances and snooker halls but that was about it. We were all from the same district and we tolerated each other. Their nemesis was the

Drimnagh crowd. Every now and then when we were hanging around our corner on the Inchicore Bridge you would see one crowd or the other. The leader of the Drimnagh crowd was called Pasty Kavanagh and his nemesis was Brendan Laird from Railway Avenue. Pasty was built like a prize fighter and he also looked like one. Brendan was very clean-cut and small in stature but one of the best fighters you could meet. He was the local boxing champion and had also boxed for St. Joseph's Club. While we never interfered with these groups on one occasion when we were at the usual corner we heard a commotion. Brendan was running up Inchicore Road, with six Drimnagh blokes in pursuit. They caught him at Kelly's pub. He was giving a good account of himself but he was also taking a lot of punishment. There were about eight of us on the corner when all of a sudden Eggo ran across the road and joined the melee. "What the hell!" Johnny shouted as the two of us responded in unison. We broke into the fight with the rest of the group following. We had them on the run with Johnny, Eggo and I in pursuit punching them as they ran. When it was over, Brendan thanked us and said, "I owe you one." Never a truer word was spoken as he eventually did repay us in a way I will relate later. Brendan made his way back to his district and we returned to our corner. A short time later, Paddy, the rest of my brothers and the usual crowd came walking down the road. We told them what had happened. Paddy wasn't happy. "What the feck are you blokes up to?" he demanded. "Don't you know we have enough trouble with the Fatima Mansions crowd. What do we do if a fight starts with the Drimnagh crowd?" He was shouting at us and we felt pretty stupid but no one said anything. I told him that we didn't like to see six fighting one. He grabbed me, which was very unusual as he never touched me, and said, "Get home." I found out later he went over to Drimnagh with his buddy Benny McDonald and made amends. We all lived far too near each other for trouble to have broken out. During this time period in the 60s, another family moved onto our road called the Dunns. There were twelve of them, and in our age group there was Herbie and his mother's brother Derrick. Both would turn out to be my life-long friends. They were originally from Church Street in Dublin. I was to spend most of my youth with this family and part of my adult life in England with them as well. Herbie was the eldest, with five younger sisters and four younger brothers. Derrick, whose nickname was Fagin, was about a year older. His father, Big Herbie as we called him, was a really nice person, his mother Maggie was a rough and tough individual with a heart of gold. They lived next doors to Bud's family. Bud was nowhere to be found since he and his Fatima Mansions crowd had beaten Georgie. We thought that was the end of him in Inchicore but we were wrong. Christie Boyle and Jimmy Anders were on O'Connell Street when they were accosted by Bud and his mates who beat up Inchicore blokes again. When we heard about it we decided to pay them a visit in Fatima Mansions. Before this could happen we had a visit from the Fatima Mansions gang, who came to Inchicore. Most of our group was at work and missed them but the Fatima crowd did meet Herbie and Derrick and beat them up. Paddy decided to call everyone together and plan strategy. Eggo, Johnny and I tried to join in but they sent us away saying we were too young. The next time the Mansions' crowd came into Inchicore everyone had to be ready. We had our own distinct whistle and even to this day if somebody gives this whistle we respond immediately. Two weeks later it was around midnight and everyone was at home sleeping. We were awoken by stones being thrown at our back bedroom window followed by the whistle. It was Johnny Dowling who lived a few doors down from us. Paddy called out, "What's happening?" Johnny was hyper. "Come on down. There are about 100 Mansions blokes in Inchicore looking for us." It turned out there were half this amount, as usual Johnny had exaggerated. With that Paddy, Jerry and Tony were up getting dressed. I was also getting dressed and when Paddy noticed this he told me to go back to sleep. They then all left the house by climbing down the drainpipe beneath the window. I watched them go over the back wall and then I jumped out of bed, got dressed and quickly followed behind them. What I was to witness that night was the biggest gang fight I had ever seen. I made my way down the back lane to Jamestown Road. As I came out of the entry there was a crowd of our blokes assembling on the corner, Paddy and the rest of my brothers among them. "Has anyone seen the Fatima Mansions gang yet?" someone asked. "I think they are in Ring Street," was the reply. With that we made our way to Ring Street. I stayed at the back of the crowd, as I did not want Paddy to see me. We crossed the Goat fields and when we came out onto Nash Street a crowd was on the corner. I recognized about twelve of them as Brendan's pals. He asked what the problem was. When one of our lads explained, Brendan and his pals decided to join us as he said he owed us one. We made our way across Railway Avenue where there was a large open field. That is when we spotted them. They were shouting, breaking bottles and making a real racket, and most of them had had too much to drink. When they caught sight of us, both gangs ran at each other with Paddy leading the charge. The leader of the Fatima gang was called Chinney O'Brien, and Paddy caught him a beautiful punch in the mouth. Chinney went down quickly. There were bodies tumbling everywhere. Bud was seen in the crowd and Jimmy Anders called to Georgie to point Bud out. When Georgie spotted Bud he made a beeline for him catching him by the neck, and punching him silly. By now it was turning into a real riot. One fellow from Fatima Mansions had barbed wire around his hand and he was using it as a knuckle duster, so of course when he punched one of our lads he cut his hand to ribbons. By now people where coming out of their houses trying to break it up. There must have been more than 100 people in the melee. I was still at the back of the crowd when I got a glimpse of my brother

Tony. One big bloke had him by the neck and Tony was taking some punishment. They both were rolling on the ground with this bloke's knee holding Tony's arms. He was bending over Tony butting him in the face. Tony was bleeding a lot so I lost my temper and made a run to where they were struggling to get through the crowd. I punched the bloke to try to get him off Tony. He didn't budge. When I looked down Tony's face was a mess. I caught the bloke by the hair and by his nose and yanked. He fell over with a yell. Tony was up like lightening and sorry to say the two of us bashed him. We did not usually interfere when it was one on one, but the bloke was big. The fighting still raged on all over the field, Tony told me to get lost and go home. I went to the outskirts of the crowd and watched, it was a massacre. Some of the Fatima Mansions crowd ran off, but the main crowd would not run. They where taking a beating but they where also inflicting a beating on some of our blokes. A lot of people were badly hurt and some knocked out. Bud was one of them. Paddy was everywhere throwing punches. You could not hear yourself think with all the noise when all of a sudden somebody shouted, "Police!" Everyone stopped abruptly and then scattered as about twenty police emerging on us from two sides. I ran with the main crowd up towards the Goatfields. People made their way in all different directions trying to get away. I found myself running up and along the canal. I dove down the embankment at the Third Lock and hid under one of the bridges. It was not long before I heard someone running. It was Jimmy Anders. He stopped to catch his breath and he was bleeding from a head wound. I was just about to call out to him to hide when all at once a policeman on a bike cornered him. He had

Jimmy against the wall of the Lock and had blocked him in with his bike. I was just about 10 feet away lying on my stomach and my heart was pounding. I don't know how they did not hear me. "Where are you coming from bowsie?" the policeman asked Jimmy." From church," Jimmy replied." And I supposed you cut your forehead when you knelt down?" "Then you must have seen what happened if you were there," Jimmy replied. "You cheeky bastard," the policeman said, "We'll see how smart you are when you are in a cell." Before the policeman could say another word Jimmy kicked his bike back, knocking the policeman over and ran up the canal and was over the loch before the man had recovered. I lay in hiding listening to the policeman swearing at what he would do to Jimmy if he ever caught sight of him again. As everything quieted down, I hid for fifteen minutes before I made my way home up

Jamestown Road and into the back entry where I climbed over my back wall. The house was silent as I climbed up the back drain spout and squeezed through the window. None of my brothers were in. I tossed and turned with worry about them until I fell into a fitful sleep. I awoke the next morning and they still had not returned. I lay there and was trying to think what I would tell Mam and Dad when I went down to breakfast. They wanted to know where my brothers were. "I think they got up early and went swimming up the canal," I replied. This seemed to satisfy them and I gulped my breakfast down, had a wash and made my way to our usual haunts looking for them. I looked everywhere but couldn't find them. I eventually made my way down to the snooker halls and low and behold, it was like a reunion. Everyone was there including my three brothers. I was so happy to see that they were all right, cut and bloodied but well. Everyone was in great spirits. I told them what had happened to Jimmy Anders and everyone started laughing. They didn't know where Jimmy was but he made it home okay. It certainly was a night to remember.

After this incident, things became very quiet in Inchicore with only the odd skirmish, rumour had it that Bud and a crowd from Fatima Mansions had gone to England to work. We didn't see them around and so we assumed that they really had left. In later years I did run into Bud in London, which is a story I will tell later on. There was a local dance hall just a few miles from Inchicore called the Mayfair. There were dances Friday, Saturday and Sunday and we never missed one. We used to hold our football dances there and sometimes the mothers and fathers of the lads would go. You can imagine whenever parents were present everybody was on their best behavior. Because it was the 60s, and there were a lot of show bands in Dublin at this time. Some of them went on to international fame. We also had a vocal group called the Bachelors who were very successful. One of our lads from Bluebell, Tommy Hendricks, fancied himself as a singer and everyone would egg him on and ask the dance announcer to call his name to sing.

When his name was called we all would cheer and he would swagger onto the stage. He would sing and sway like Elvis and everyone always enjoyed his antics. There used to be talent contests once a month and Tommy would to win them all, not because he was the best but because he put his heart and soul into his performances.

One Saturday night the papers advertised a talent contest in a dance hall in Ballsbridge, a posh suburb of

Dublin. We all decided to enter Tommy, more for a lark than anything else.

About thirty of us arrived at the dance hall on the night of the contest. It was not the usual crowd that frequented this dance hall. For starters, nearly everyone had a car and we were lucky if we had a bike. They all seemed quite well off. There was some terrific talent but we were all waiting for Tommy to perform. Of course when his name was called we were shouting and cheering. I don't think the local crowd was used to this unruly behaviour. Tommy climbed onto the stage. He wore a powder blue suit with a velvet collar, drainpipe trousers and thick soled shoes with a red cravat around his neck. He was like something a dog would drag home, but full of confidence. He was also very drunk. By now we were uncontrollable with laughter. The fact he was He taking himself so seriously just added to our mirth. Tommy was introduced as the best singer in Inchicore (not saying much for the real singers from our district).

He took the microphone in his hand and before he sang he said, "I would like to dedicate this song to a very special person who is in the audience tonight, Mary O'Rourke."

Mary was one of our crowd and she nearly died with embarrassment. Tommy was crazy about her but she could not stand him. "Tell that stupid git to shut up," she said. Of course this made us start laughing again. Tommy sang an Elvis song "Don't step on my Blue Suede Shoes." He gave it all he had, gyrating his hips, shaking his knees and kneeling on the stage. When he was finished he had the whole of the dance hall in hysterics as they had never seen anything like this. When it came time to pick the winner there was thunderous applause for Tommy. He was not the best singer but he surely was the best entertainer. When the judge was presenting Tommy with his prize (ten pounds and 200 cigarettes) Tommy said he had to sing one more song. He said it was a dedication to his life and the song was Frank Sinatra's "My Way." Again we burst into laughter, what a bloke. By the time the dance was over and Johnny, Eggo, Tommy and I were in the crowd outside, it was 1 a.m.. We had no way of getting home but to walk. We were talking to a group from the dance when they started throwing their keys to each other. Tommy disappeared for a time and then suddenly drove up in a beautiful car, flashing his lights at us. "Get in quickly," he said. We all piled in and away he drove. "Where did you get this car?" we asked. "Some ejit was throwing his keys and I grabbed them, and here we are." How we got home is still a mystery to me. We parked the car in a car park in Inchicore and Tommy treated us all to fish and chips. It was another night I will never forget.

Another time at the Mayfair I was with a friend of mine from Ballyfermot. Noel Rush was on leave from the British Army and we both had dates. My dates' name was Maureen Harcourt and Noel's was Carmel Mahen. We were having a quiet drink in the pub just across from the dance when suddenly there was a lot of shouting from the bar. We paid no attention but continued talking and drinking. An hour or so later we decided to go to the Mayfair but as we were walking across the road the crowd from the bar shouted remarks at us. We tried to ignore them when one of them shouted at Noel. "Hey you are the bloke that picked a fight with me last week?" The girls said, "Pay no attention," but this was advice Noel didn't take. He shouted back,

"If you don't go home I will pick on you again." Of course Noel had never seen these people before. I nearly died. Here we were two of us to nearly twenty of them. By this time we were just outside the Mayfair when they surrounded us. Noel and I stood together in the middle of this crowd. Noel whispered," We will be bashed here, but at least let's go for the big mouth that's shouting at us." With that said we both grabbed the bloke and before the crowd could stop us we walloped him. Then suddenly we were punched and kicked from every angle. The girls tried to help but they also were hurt. It was over as quick as it had started. We were both in bits but Noel was worse than I as his front tooth was broken. The girls were hysterical. We all cooled down and made our way into the dance hall. The doorman was not letting us enter but relented when the girls started crying. We washed up as best we could. By now our crowd had heard about our mishap and they went looking for that gang to no avail. We never met this gang again as we took leave of each other that night and I caught the bus to Inchicore with Maureen. We arrived at her house in Kilmainham and when her father saw her he went crazy. I tried to explain but he would not listen. Maureen had a swollen lip and looked awful. He told me if ever he caught me with his daughter again he would not be responsible for his actions, and with that he sent me packing. As the old saying goes, "Another fine mess I got myself into." So much for the start of my love life.

However, I did meet Maureen some weeks later and again I started to date her, which we did for quite a while until I left for England. Of course she never did tell her father it was me she was dating.

CHAPTER 9

I was finished school now and I was working in a chemical factory in Island Bridge. It was a terrific job and I enjoyed the crowd that worked there. I even made another life-long friend, Noel Maguire. Mr. Finn was the caretaker and he had a house down by the Liffey. He was a great old character, very Dublin-like and down to earth. Our boss was an ex Royal Air Force Pilot named Boyes, a true gentleman. Noel and I were the dog's bodies, and used to do all the odd jobs around the factory. We used to sneak out everyday in the summer and swim the river Liffey, and also have a pint of Guinness in the pub across the road. One fond memory I have is of the manager's son visiting one day, (he was about seven years of age). In his gruff Dublin voice Mr. Finn asked him," What's your name son?" "Basil," was the reply. "And do you go to school?" "Yes sir." "And what are they teaching you?" "Elocution lessons sir." With that Mr. Finn turned to me and said, "These fecking kids nowadays know too much." Mr. Finn was funny. He used to shout at Noel all the time about not doing his work. Noel used to pretend on he couldn't hear him. This went on for some time until eventually Finn was fed up and called him into his little office. He handed Noel the bus fare to attend the hospital for a hearing test. Noel was delighted to have some time off. At the hospital they removed the wax from his ears and he was never able to pretend he couldn't hear again. I was still at loose ends as most of my friends were eighteen and leaving home to go to England, so I decided to go also. I told my mother that I was leaving and she was extremely upset. As I was only 16 years of age, she would not let me go. I told her if she objected I would run away and with that she relented, but only if I would go to my brother Tony who lived in Luton. I agreed. It was sad saying my good-byes, but at this point everybody made for England. Another friend, Kevin Dowls, decided to go with me.

When I arrived in England I had thirty shillings in my pocket. We arrived in London on a very foggy day and Kevin said, "Bernie, what the feck are we doing here?" I just smiled and replied, "I'm here for the spas." Our money soon ran out and we were very hungry. We slept rough in St. James Park and underneath the embankment. We soon got to know the local down and outs. We looked for work but to no avail. Things were getting desperate when we decided to go to Watford, a suburb of London where Kevin's brother lived. We jumped a train as we had no money for fare. We entered one of the carriages and lo and behold there was a woman's handbag on the seat that some poor soul had forgotten. Kevin whipped it open and there were 3 pounds and some change—this was a Godsend. When we arrived in Watford, we found a cafe and we had the best fish and chips we had ever tasted. We were feeling much better. We arrived at Kevin's brother digs but he was not at home. We went down to his local and inquired about him. The locals were looking at us funny. One big bloke walked over to us. "Are you blokes looking for trouble and why do you want Pasty?" When we explained who we were his attitude changed and he sent over two pints—these were friends of Patsy's. Eventually he came into the bar and was he surprised to see us. He put us both up and he looked after us very well. We both got jobs in Watford but they did not last long. We decided to go to Luton in Bedfordshire, where we knew our entire old crowd was living, Paddy, Gerry and Tony. Kevin got digs in Leighton Buzzard a few miles from Luton. I got digs in a cafe on Leegrove road with my brother Tony and Hen Doyle. My first priority was to find a job, which I did in the local bakery, called the Coop Bakery. It was the hardest job l ever had. I started work at 6 a.m. and worked between two massive ovens putting dough in to bake the bread. The heat was unbelievable, but a job was a job. My weekly wage was 6 pound 10 shillings—I was rich. Johnny Anders also came to live in Luton as he had a brother that was living there. It was great to see him again.

We all used to go into the George Hotel Pub and all the gang from Inchicore used to congregate there. Most of them were employed at Vauxhall Motors. I never fancied working there as I couldn't see myself working on a line. I enjoyed living in my digs at Leegrove Road, as I met many people there. A motorcycle crowd used to frequent the cafe and I got to know them very well, which was good because they were a very wild bunch and you know the old saying, "never make an enemy when you can make a friend."

Life was good in this little hamlet but by now I was beginning to get the wanderlust so I decided to leave Luton for greener pastures wherever they may be.
Johnny decided to go with me. Two blokes, Freddie McGavan and Ernie Marsh, who where also from our district at home, joined us. We said our good-byes but Tony whom I was in digs with did not like the idea. He had taken on the responsibility for me, you know big brothers. I was 17 by now and I thought I knew it all. However, nothing could deter me and the four of us

caught the bus to Welwyn Garden City. It was a nice town so we decided to stay, but alas, we did not fare well in this town as there was no work and our money soon dwindled. Once again we were sleeping rough without food. I remember one night in particular, when we were sleeping outside of town under a bridge. It was very cold and we were trying to heat our hands on the light fixture underneath the bridge. We were like this for a few weeks living from hand to mouth, pinching food where we could. There was an apple orchard we used to rob and fill ourselves up with the fruit. We were constantly being moved by the police wherever we tried to sleep, so we finally decided to leave and go to Stevenage in Hertfordshire. Still, we had no luck. Johnny and I were talking about going home or trying to make a go of it. We decided to join the army as we thought that was a better alternative than starving. Ernie and Freddie decided they would join us. We found the local recruiting office and entered very nervously. The recruiting sergeant handed us some forms to fill in and when we were finished we noticed Ernie looked very nervous. Suddenly he said "Feck you blokes," and ran from the office. Freddie took off after him. Johnny and I were starting to have second thoughts. The sergeant came out and asked what was happening and where our friends had gone. We told him they had changed their minds, which we also wanted to do. How to do it, however, was another matter. Johnny whispered to me," I'm not going. I don't want to end up in fecking Borneo."

The sergeant came and took our applications when Johnny asked about the pay. When the sergeant told us how low it was, Johnny said, "Sorry I was expecting more," and with that he walked out, leaving me sitting there in turmoil. "What about you?" the sergeant asked. "What are you going to do?" I gave the stupidest reply, "I have to ask my father." Before he could answer and with a look of surprise on his face I left. Johnny was outside laughing. So much for our army life. We met up with Freddie and Ernie in town and decided to hitchhike to London to see if we would fare any better there. We split up to have a better chance of a lift. Freddie and Ernie went off in one direction and Johnny and I stuck together. Arrangements were made to meet in Ealing Broadway. It was a lovely day when we started hitchhiking and we soon got a lift from a truck driver for about twenty miles before he turned off in another direction. As we carried on to London on foot, the weather was changing and it started raining heavily. We were in an awful way. It was dark now and there was not much chance of catching another ride, so we started to look for a dry place to sleep. We eventually found one in an old castle ruin, in one room there was an overhang, so at least we would not get wet. We spent the most miserable of nights, sleeping and waking throughout night with hunger pains. When we woke at dawn it was misty and still drizzling so we just sat there to keep out of the rain. About 10 a.m. it cleared up and we continued on our journey.

We were walking for about an hour or so and the hunger was getting unbearable. We came across a small cafe and decided to get something to eat. We ordered a meal which we both devoured and then ordered seconds that we also finished off in record time. Then the two of us sat there waiting for the first opportunity to make our escape, as we had not a penny between us. We watched the owner cook. He suddenly went out of a door to the back of the cafe when we bolted for the door like lightening. We must have run for four miles before we stopped. Johnny said, "That was very fine dining. The next time we pass this hamlet we must do lunch." With that we both started laughing. Eventually we made it to Ealing Broadway, but there was no sign of Freddie and Ernie and again we had to find somewhere to sleep. The local park was our next bed. The weather was good and we both had park benches to sleep on. Ealing Broadway is a busy little town and we set out to look for a job but in our state we had no luck. As we were wondering around, I found some postal orders, some of which were signed and some not. We tried to cash them in two shops with no luck but we eventually found one shop that did cash one of them for 35 shillings—we were in the money. We dined well at a local fish and chip shop and also bought some potato-chips for our supper, and then we made our way to our abode in the park. We settled down for the night and were eating our chips. "Bernard we have to watch our calories. Overeating is bad for us, two meals in one day is obesity," said Johnny. He always had a great sense of humor. The next day we met Ernie in town on his own. He was delighted to see us. Freddie had gone his separate way. "Thank God I met you blokes," he said. "This fellow has been shadowing me all day. I think he loves me." We all smiled.

Freddie and Ernie had also had a meal in a cafe without paying. "What a wonderful country, free meals and lodgings," I said. With that we all laughed. The three of us were not doing very well so we decided to call my brother Joey who was in the Royal Air Force (RAF).

Joey had left home when I was quite young and I did not really know him very well as he rarely came home. He was stationed in Hendon, one of the RAF bases, and was completely surprised to here from me. He arranged to meet us at Hyde Park corner at midnight. He had to make some arrangements and it was the soonest he could see us. At 12 on the dot we three were at Hyde Park comer. Joey drove up in a minivan and was delighted to see me, but also mad at me for getting myself into this state. However, I didn't think I was in a state as I was enjoying myself. He took us for a meal at one of the food vans that were everywhere in London at night, hot-dogs covered in onions — gourmet food indeed. Joey took me aside to talk to me and asked me what my plans were. "To get a job," I replied. He wanted me to get rid of Ernie and Johnny as he did not know them but I refused. He had to report back to his base and gave me some money and told me to keep in touch and phone him in a few days. I promised I would. We slept in the park again that night after another fine day of dining.

The next day we started to look for work in earnest. I got a job in Victoria painting council houses and also some digs. Johnny got a job in Shepherd's Bush and Ernie decided to go back to Dublin. I job was painting for the local council so I was outside working, but alas it did not last long and again I found myself jobless and alone as Johnny had moved to Shepherd's Bush. I phoned Joey. He had a flat in Sussex Gardens, Paddington. He picked me up and brought me to the smallest flat I had ever seen. It had one bed and about 2 ft of space in between. I stayed there that night but there was no way he could put me up. However, he brought me down to the west end the next day and got me a job in the Nuffield Center where he used to work there part time. He also got me a flat in Fulham and life was good again.

CHAPTER 10

The Nuffield Center was subsidized by the Lord Nuffield Association and it served the Forces of the crown. I spent two years working there and it was one of the most enjoyable experiences I ever had. There was an audition room that the BBC used to use, a massive dining room, a dance hall, a barber shop and a large bar. I used to get free haircuts and food and see lots of famous actors coming in and out for auditions with the BBC. The Nuffield Center was situated near St. Martin in the Fields, Trafalgar Square, Charing Cross and the Strand right in the middle of a very exciting district. I made a lot of new friends— young and old. One friend in particular named Bob, once owned a bar at the seaside in Margate, but he drank heavily, was divorced—a real down and out character. The Nuffield used to employ a lot of casual labour in the kitchens during busy periods and many characters passed through, including many unemployed actors. It was never boring. I picked up a lot of bad habits. I started drinking around the Strand in a pub called the Long Bar, supposedly the longest bar in Britain. I very seldom used to get to my flat in Fulham as it was quite a distance from Trafalgar Square to home. My leisure time was spent in the Black and White cafe and the other pubs on the Strand. A lot of my friends were in the Coldstream, Irish and Scots Guards, as Buckingham Palace was just on Whitehall. Also there was another guards Barracks in Chelsea. On one occasion I was out drinking with my buddies, who were staying in the Union Jack Club that was only for soldiers. It was late so they invited me back to sleep at their place. It was terrific. I had something to eat and was settling down on a nice sofa to sleep.

Just as I was dozing off, I was awoken by the doorman who asked for my identification. Of course I was turned out. I ended up asleep in the back of a British Rail Truck in Waterloo railway station. The next morning I woke with the truck driving up the Strand and I jumped out at the first traffic lights. What a night. When I had no money I used to go to Paddington to see my brother Joey. He wasn't usually in so I would sleep in the little garden in front of his house. Around 4 a.m. the milk trucks used to pass. I would hide myself on the comer and whenever the trucks had to stop at the traffic lights, I would to pinch two pints of milk from the back for my breakfast. Generally when you slept outside out and roughed it, your senses were always alert for any opportunity to survive I was always on the look out for a safe place to sleep, and I do that even to this day wherever I am. Every other week I used to visit my brother in Luton, 7 shillings and 6 pence return. I used to stay for the weekend but by now most of our crowd had gone back to London and my brothers were about to depart also. I was very happy to hear this as I missed them. When all of the old crowd was settled back in London in a district called the Angel, I would visit them and recall this incident. In the bar where they drank, a bloke was beaten up and a glass broken over his head. His friends came into the bar looking for whoever did it. None of our lads had anything to do with it, but these individuals were looking for trouble. This one big bloke asked to fight the hardest individual in the bar and described what he was going to do to the bloke who beat up his friend. There were seven of us sitting having a pint, two of my brothers, Tony and Gerry. Also Georgie, Jimmy

Anders, Hen and Maurice Gibb who were boyhood friends from Dublin. Hen said to Maurice, "Go ahead, take his challenge." Maurice smiled. "Do you dare me?" he asked. "Yes." With that Maurice said to the bloke," Will I do?" The bloke was amazed as Maurice was dwarfed by him. "Go home," he said. With that Maurice hit him and knocked him out cold. Everyone was delighted as his buddy just carried him out and that was that. I only used my flat in Fulham to sleep when I made it home, which was very seldom. When you are having a good time, you don't want to go home. The nights I did sleep out I had special places: Charing Cross Station was the best, though I was were moved quite often. Hungerford Alley and the Arches were also good places where you able to keep dry. Mick's all-night cafe on Fleet Street, underneath the embankment, was another good place. I knew most of the street people and what a mosaic of people they were. The stories of how they became down and out are too numerous to mention. Some names have stuck in my memory such as Mongo, and Ted the Head, who had a habit of butting anyone who disagreed with him. Another person was Half a Steak, who was known to order steak and chips and run out without paying, leaving half a steak on his plate. Most of the street people were people who used to drink too much and of course this had caused them trouble—broken marriages and so forth. Apart from this, they were wonderful characters and made my life on the streets very enjoyable. You could meet any one of them in the places I have mentioned and they were always the first to share what little they had. Their first priority of any day was having enough money to get a wash and brush up. I suppose by doing this they fantasized they were not really down and out. When Mongo needed money he used to stand in the subway station and sing at the top of his voice. I think people gave him money to be quiet because he had a most unusual craggy voice, in fact, it was awful. However, he did make money and when Mongo made money we all ate very well as he was a very generous person. Ted The Head played the mouth organ and he used to busk in Piccadilly Circus. He also made money but sadly Ted drank all of it away. He was always ending up in hospital, but always managed to survive. I was sleeping rough one night in St. James Park on a bench. I was woken up by someone going through my pockets. There were two of them. What a joke, the blind robbing the blind. These two were not the usual down and outs and were shouting at me to give them money. Looking back I think they were probably on drugs, which was unusual for this period. I kicked one of them on the knee and he fell to the ground. The second one grabbed me around the neck and we both rolled onto the ground. By now, the first one held my feet and I was afraid for my life. Suddenly Ted the Head appeared from out of the blue. He kicked one of them on the chest and between the two of us we made short work of them. Thank God for Ted the Head. Looking back at this period in my life I would not have changed one iota of anything that I did and will always look back with nostalgia at the friends I made. I thank them all and hope that most of them did well when I departed from this little corner of London.

CHAPTER 11

I was at loose ends going from job to job. I was employed at Lyons Tea in Hammersmith. I was in the section that made Christmas puddings and meat pies. It was a massive complex and I was situated in the underground part of the factory. One day as I was on my way to break, I was walking along this corridor when these two blokes passed me. One seemed very familiar. We both turned and recognized each other immediately. It was my old and dear friend Derrick Fagin from Dublin. He had left Dublin some years ago to live in Huddersfield, it must have some five years since I had last seen him. You can imagine the surprise and happiness I felt when we met. We both shook hands vigorously. "Derrick my old friend what are you doing here?" I asked. He introduced me to his pal Alex McSheffrey from Londonderry. Alex was small of stature but very stocky. They were both down from Huddersfield doing some construction work at the factory. What a small world, I thought to myself. I never imagined I'd meet Derrick again. I arranged to meet both of them after work in a pub in Shepherds Bush. They both had digs near there. When I arrived at the pub called the Bush Hotel it was like stepping into my local pub in Dublin. I met blokes I used to go to school with, also there was quite a crowd from Ballyfermet that I used to play soccer against. Derrick and Alex were there and I can tell you many a pint was hoisted that night. It was terrific to be with old friends again. Our meetings were much the same over the next three months. Derrick and Alex's jobs were finishing and they were to return to Huddersfield in two weeks time. I felt sad, as we had grown very close. I arranged to meet them for a farewell drink in the Bush a couple of days before they were to leave. It was much the same when I entered the pub as it was the first time, the Ballyfermet crowd was exchanging a few pleasantries, but you could not hear yourself talk as the music was very loud. At about 10 p.m. as I was having my pint with Derrick and Alex and reminiscing when lo and behold in walked Bud Collins and the Fatima Mansion crowd, every one of them in Teddy Boy outfits. Derrick and I nearly died as they were our mortal enemies.

"Let's get the feck out of here," Derrick whispered to me, as we both knew we would be battered if they spotted us. Of course it was already too late.

"What have we here," Bud said as he approached our table. Alex knew something was wrong as he saw our faces. I think it was the face of fear, and the pints we drank that night did not give us courage.

"Hello Bud," Derrick replied "I hope you are well and would you have a pint with us?"

"I don't drink with shit heads," Bud answered and with that everyone at our table tensed. They were beginning to feel something was not right.

"Feck off Bud," Derrick replied. "Let's not have any trouble, just sit down and have a pint."

"I said I don't drink with shitheads," Bud replied. With that Bud's crowd started to move towards our table and there were a couple of noted scrappers from Dublin with him. In fact, some of them still had the scars from past confrontations with the Inchicore crowd. We all came to our feet. There was only six of us and about twenty of them. I thought we were in for a licking. By now the pub was very quiet. Derrick again said, "Look Bud have a drink and sit down." I must add that in the last five years Derrick had worked on construction sites and had developed a powerful build. Bud punched at Derrick and caught him on the side of the head. When the punch was thrown two of the blokes at our table ran for the door. We did not know them very well so we understood. We were trapped in a corner. We were giving a good account of ourselves for the moment as Bud's crowd could not get at us; we were pushing tables and chairs in all directions. Surprisingly, the Ballyfermot crowd came to our assistance led by Willow Maher and some of my school chums. It wasn't long before we got the upper hand. I made a beeline for Bud and caught him a beautiful right on the side of his head, and he dropped. By now Derrick was surprising a lot of people by his prowess as a scrapper. I had never seen anything like it— when he hit someone they went down. By now the police had arrived and we all scattered in every direction. Alex, Derrick and I got away out of the back and ran down Shepherd's Bush to Hammersmith, never stopping to look back. We were elated, our adrenaline high, at the prospect of beating Bud. We went into the Black & White Cafe at Hammersmith Broadway and had a cup of tea and said our good-byes. As we were sitting Derrick said to me, "Bernard why don't you come back with us to Huddersfield?" I don't know why I said I would. Maybe it was the alcohol or my adrenaline still pumping, two days later we where changing trains at Doncaster bound for Huddersfield.

When we arrived in Huddersfield it was a culture shock from London. They still had trams for buses and there were a lot of derelict buildings, but it was a quaint town and I grew to love it. We got lodgings at Greenhead Park and settled in. It was a nice old house but paying the rent every week with the three of us not working was very difficult. Derrick and Alex had some family there so they helped us a lot but many a time we would go hungry. I was reacquainted with my old friend Herbie Dunn and some of the crowd from Jamestown Avenue. It was grand to see them again and they also helped us. We used to go into the local fish and chip shop and ask for the batter that was left in the tray, that's how hungry we were. Eventually we all found jobs, Derrick and Alex in construction and I as a bus conductor, so things brightened up considerably. As time went by I got to know the local crowd and used to go to all the dances and jazz clubs. Life was good and I was really appreciating Yorkshire. The people were terrific and I made many new friends. I was at a dance one night when I met this girl. I was getting on great with her and 1 asked to take her home.

She agreed but said that she lived quite a distance. "No problem," I replied. We left and got the bus from the local terminal and an hour and fifteen minutes later we arrived out in the country. We walked up and down country lanes and hills for a further forty minutes until we arrived at her house that was on a little farm. We made a date for the following Friday, kissed goodnight and she was gone. There I was at 2 a.m. in the middle of nowhere. Smart hey! I walked back over fields, bogs, and streams. What a state I was in. Purely by luck at about 7:30 a.m. a milk truck picked me up and gave me a ride into town. I got lots of strange looks as I walked back to my lodgings and when I walked into our room Derrick and Alex were having breakfast. They looked at me and started to laugh, I mean *really* laugh, then I looked into the mirror and saw why. I was covered in shit. I new my shoes and clothes were mucky but so were my face and hair. I had taken a couple of tumbles on the way back but I didn't realize how bad I looked. I had a wash and fell into bed—what a night!

The following Friday we ended up at the same dance, when Derrick said "Bernard your girlfriend is here." I'm afraid I took the coward's way out and avoided her. I didn't fancy another nightmare walk as I was just getting over the last one.

One night Alex, Derrick, Alex's brother and I were in a country pub in the Yorkshire dales. We were drinking and singing and having a good time with the locals when I did a very stupid thing. I had some fire crackers and I threw one under some stools where a crowd of people were seated. Of course when it went up pints were upset, people jumped up wondering what had happened. Needless to say they didn't see the funny side and we barely made it out of town alive. The crowd turned on us and we legged it to Alex's brother's car. We were lucky to get away as there were some extremely large farmers in the throng. Derrick and the lads gave out hell to me, sorry.

By this time I was beginning to get the roaming bug in me again and I decided to leave Huddersfield and return to Dublin. It was sad leaving Derrick and Alex as they were true friends, and little did I know I would not hear from Derrick again for twenty-eight years. *Dear Reader I would like to jump ahead with my story, to finish this period of my life.* The next time I heard from Derrick was through a phone call one evening to my home in Canada. It was Christmas Eve and I had some friends over for a Christmas drink. My son said there was a phone call for me. It was my dear old friend Derrick and I was delighted to hear from him. Seemingly, he had met my brother when he was in Dublin on vacation and my brother gave him my phone number. We caught up on old times and he invited me to his 25th wedding anniversary the following May. Of course I flew over to England in May and caught a train to a town called Siddal in Halifax were Derrick and his daughter met me at the station. He had not changed a bit to me. We clasped hands and were both delighted to see each other. I stayed in his house where his lovely wife Annette made me very comfortable. I had a marvelous time at their party where I renewed old friendships. Herbie was there, he was now a grandfather (how the years fly by) along with all the old crowd from Dublin. What a time we had. When it was time to return home, Derrick was crying. Parting was terrible. We kept in touch with numerous phone calls promising to meet again with our wives for a holiday, but the plans of "mice and men" never did happen. On New Year's night at around 12:30 I received a call from Annette. I knew before I took up the phone that something was wrong. I said "hello" and there was silence. Annette finally said, "Bernard tonight when Derrick came home from his club he collapsed and died from a brain hemorrhage." I mumbled some words of condolence, forget what I said. I sat up all night. I could not believe it, he was only fifty. I suppose I will never really get over it, my boyhood pal, my adult friend, my brother was dead. May God bless and keep him for I will miss him forever. I still keep in touch with Annette with a card and phone calls. Annette, my deepest sympathies for I know you loved him very much.

Footnote: Herbie is also dead, another friend dying too

young and another part of my life gone. I travel every year to the Yorkshire Dales for a couple of days and travel around by car. It is the most beautiful place on earth to me and they are both in my thoughts. Goodbye dear friends until we meet again.

CHAPTER 12

I arrived back in Dublin dressed to the nines. (I think if I was chocolate I would have eaten myself). I renewed my acquaintance with Johnny and Eggo who were delighted to see me. I had never kept in touch and we all had a lot of making up to do. Eggo was just back from Birmingham and Johnny from London we were all drinking at Clearys on the back road in Inchicore so most of the crowd was there. My brother Paddy just lived across the road from Clearys in a little cottage. He heard that I was back and he came over to the pub. It was terrific to see him he was just the same lovable character. Most of the crowd was employed in a steel works in Clondalkin in County Dublin. My brothers Paddy and Jerry were also employed there so they got me a job.

I was the youngest employee at the steel works so it was left to me to run around for everyone, getting sandwiches and tea and also to do all the menial jobs. But that was okay as I enjoyed it, especially with all our crowd working there. I must mention this one occurrence that happened when I was employed there. About six weeks into my new job four detectives drove through the gates one day. I saw them arrive and go into the manager's office. After about fifteen minutes I was called into the office, my heart was in my mouth, there were these four big individuals glaring at me.

"What have you got to say for yourself and why did you do it?" they asked.

I had no clue as to what they were talking about but they kept repeating, "Why did you do it?" This kept going for about half an hour and I was beginning to get annoyed. When for the 50th time they asked, "Why did you do it?" I shouted, "What the feck did I do?" At last they told me what had happened. Some toffs had been in touch with them about a smash and grab on a jeweler's shop in Huddersfield. Toffs was the name the Irish police called the English police. Anyway, they caught one of the culprits and he had given my name as an accomplice. I was flabbergasted as I had never done anything like this. I still did not know why anyone would accuse me. I suppose whoever did it knew me and as I had left Huddersfield they thought that I would be safe and they would protect the real accomplice. I told the police it was not me, but they wouldn't believe me, and I was beginning to be afraid. Suddenly the office door banged open and Paddy appeared. He was furious at the police for questioning me alone and he told them so. Paddy identified himself to them and asked what I had done. When they explained, Paddy turned to me and asked, "Did you do it Bernard?"

"Absolutely not," I replied, and with that Paddy said,

"End this interrogation now or charge him." They did not charge me and as they were leaving they told me they would be back after some more investigations.

They never did come back and life returned to normal once again.

Another part of my job was working in the security shed shipping ingots, which were white metal and very expensive. The manager used to look at me funny after that police visit as if I was a big-time criminal. I also noticed the security man at the gate watching me. I suppose they had connected me in their minds to the police visit and people say, "there is no smoke without fire," but to this day I still don't now what happened. I continued to work at the metal works for another nine months, until I was truly fed up. One day as I left the job to get the blokes their lunches, I went into the local pub called Palmers. There I met a few buddies and one pint led to another. To cut a long story short, when I returned to work I quit because I had already decided to leave Ireland and return to England. Again it was sad saying my good-byes, but little did I realize that this would be the last time I would ever live in Ireland.

My destination was Birmingham and another bloke from the steel works named John Delany had decided to come with me. That was what it was like in Ireland at that time. At the drop of a hat people would leave their friends and relations at a moment's notice.

We arrived in New Street Station on a beautiful summer's day. We had no knowledge of the geography of Birmingham so we caught the first bus that came along and landed in a small town called Ballsal Heath. Our first impression of this town was not good so we made our way up the main road for a mile or so and stopped at a small cafe for a meal. There were some bus conductors in a cafe who told us there were jobs on the buses. We left our luggage at the cafe and made our way to the bus recruiting centre where we were hired immediately. They told us to report two days later for training. We couldn't believe our luck in getting a job in such a short time. Our next concern was to find digs, which we did on Station Road, Kingsheath, a very nice part of town about two miles from Ballsal Heath where our jobs were. We soon settled down to our new life and everything was fine. My route as a bus conductor took me from Kingsheath downtown to a place called the Bullring, or Spaghetti Junction as it was known locally.

John didn't last long on the buses as he got caught up with a real low-life bunch of people who dealt in drugs. They were a mean bunch of Birmingham and Dublin blokes who were led by a Scottish guy. I stayed away and I told John to do the same, but to no avail. He soon left the digs and moved to Ballsal Heath. I enjoyed working in Birmingham and met some very good friends (John and Terry). In fact, I would like to relate an incident about how I was saved from a beating or worse about six months after John left our digs. It was a Saturday night and I was with a crowd from the bus station when we decided to go for a drink at a pub in Ballsal Heath. It was a real dump but we went in. John Delaney was in there with his new crowd. I went over and said hello and he was pleased to see me. I knew some of the Dublin blokes he was with and we made small talk and then I returned to my friends. As the night wore on, most of my friends left and I ended up with John and company. When the time for last orders came I had two pints in front of me when this big Scottish bloke took one of my pints and started to drink it. I grabbed my pint from his hand and he was absolutely furious. "You'll never finish those pints," he said. "Feck you I will," I replied. "If you don't finish them you are in trouble," he said, and with that I turned the two pints onto the floor. He made a grab for me and I jumped up and gave him a push. All of a sudden his legs went out from under him and he fell hard. (He had slipped on the beer I had emptied.) When he recovered he told me I was "dead." He was with a large crowd and I asked John and a few of the other blokes he was with for help. The look of fright that came over their faces was my answer. I was looking for a way out and there was only one way— the back door that had a padlock on it. The Scottish fellow and about seven of his mates where blocking the front entrance. The pub was beginning to empty and I was getting a little desperate. I walked towards the door and said to the Scottish fellow, "I'll fight you alone," but he was shouting and really mad. There was one little opening between his pals and as I was arguing with him I made a run for it. My collar was grabbed but somehow I made it out of the door and ran for my life. I could hear the ground shaking behind me. I was running hard up the hill to the main road of Ballsal Heath when walking down was this little fellow from the buses. When he saw what was happening he started running with me. It would have been funny only it was so serious. They were catching up to me and I was really tired, as I came to the main road a bus was just pulling away from the stop. I was shouting for it to stop. I would never have made it but Terry was the conductor and he could see what was happening. He gave three rings and the bus stopped, both of us jumped on and fell into the seat. With us both safely on board, Terry gave another ring and we got away. What a near escape for those blokes were a mean bunch. I was never so happy to be entering my district safe and sound. I would have to be careful from now on. I later found out that the Scottish bloke was the leader of that mean bunch.

I was working away on the buses but every now and then I had the Ballsal Heath run. When I used to pass this certain part of the district I would go halfway up the stairs on my double decker bus so anyone getting on would not see me right away. For months this Scottish bloke was looking for me. I didn't think he was the forgiving type. During this period I had a letter from my brother Jerry who now lived in Ellesmere Port, Cheshire. He wrote that there was lots of work in Ellesmere Port and asked if I would be interested in coming to live there. I was at loose ends so I decided to give it a try.

I had no ties in Birmingham but I had enjoyed my brief stay and the friends I had met whom I will always remember. I left my digs and started to hitchhike to Cheshire. I was traveling through Shrewsbury, which was a beautiful town and was in the country part where my ride had dropped me off. I was getting out of his truck when he picked up another hitch and I couldn't believe it was Mick Neville, an old friend from Dublin. We said our quick hellos and he was gone. It sure is a small world. I arrived in Ellesmere Port at 5 p.m. April 1964 and little did I know this town was to become the most important destination of my life. My first impression wasn't very good. It was an very industrial town and therefore very polluted. Jerry and his wife made me very welcome and I soon had a job. Jerry was right about the work situation. Everywhere there were lots of jobs. I went from job to job until I finally settled into one job at the local dairy being a milkman. It was a job that suited me down to the ground as I was an early riser. I had always wanted to immigrate to Australia and when Gerry told me he was leaving Ellesmere Port to settle in Canada I went ahead and applied for Australia. They sent for me to have a medical in Manchester and I went for an interview and passed all the criteria for immigration. In those days it cost 10 pounds. I planned to leave in a couple of months as Jerry was leaving for Canada in a few weeks. As the time drew near for Jerry's departure a crowd of us took him out for a farewell drink to a nice pub on the outskirts of town. We had a darts tournament. There was quite a crowd of people seeing Jerry off and it was a great night. Halfway through the evening two of my friends and I went into the lounge for a quiet drink as the bar was really getting loud. It was a nice spot and we ordered our drinks and settled down. I was glancing around when across the room us I noticed a crowd of girls enjoying a celebration. I am not prone to rashness but when I looked at one of the girls it was as if I had always known her—she just looked so familiar. I think in the far reaches of your mind you always picture the girl you will marry and I was looking right at her. She had shoulder length hair that shone from across the room, a beautiful face and blue eyes. I know there are a lot of skeptics who do not believe in love at first sight but this happened to me. I could not keep my eyes off her; she had the most beautiful smile. I had dated many girls in my life but at this moment I was tongue-tied. How was I going to meet her and what would she see in the likes of me? All of these thoughts were flowing through my mind when all of a sudden one of my mates jumped up and said, "Let's go over and chat up the girls." Just like that. In no time at all he was laughing and joking with them and he called me over and introduced me. To this day with my accent and mumbling I don't know what I said. Her name was Jennifer and she had the most beautiful demeanor. Other girls were talking to me but I never heard a word. Only when Jennifer spoke did I hear. The night was coming to an end and I had to make a date with her but words escaped me and I was still tongue-tied. I felt like a real fool. They all said their good-byes and I was left standing there feeling miserable. I had lost my chance. We had another pint before closing and I could have kicked myself. I knew I would never meet anyone like Jennifer again. Jerry stuck his head in and asked if I want a ride home. I said I would walk, and as I was heading down the main road with a mate into the Port, Jennifer and her friend Averil were at a bus stop. She said hello and I asked her if she would like to go for a Chinese meal. She said okay, so the four of us went to a nearby restaurant. It was then that I realized I had no more money— I was a wreck. We sat and I ordered four glasses of milk. The waitress said, "We only serve milk with meals." I told her we would be ordering but could she bring the milk now. When I told Jennifer and Averil I had no money, they thought it was very funny but the restaurant didn't. We gulped down our milk and left. I walked Jennifer home to her door and we made arrangements to meet the following night at her house. In my job there was a foreman who was a holy terror. His name was Jack Colt. The next evening when I knocked at Jennifer's door, low and behold, who opened the door but Jack. He was really gruff and said, "What do you want?" I stammered, "I came to pick up Jennifer." "There's no Jennifer here," he replied and my face dropped. Only then did I realize I was on the wrong road. Eventually I found the right one, thank God. I went in and met her mother and father and sister— the nicest family you could ever meet. I went out steadily with Jennifer and postponed my trip to Australia. I was dating Jennifer for three months when I asked her to marry me. I also told her I would like to emigrate and to my surprise and delight she told me "I'll go where you go." I was never more surprised at her answer and we were married in 1966 in the Catholic Church in Ellesmere Port. We emigrated to Canada six months later, (we decided it was a bit closer than Australia) where we still live to this day.

I often go over to England and Dublin, and when I am in Dublin I never fail to walk from Inchicore down the back road to Kilmainham to Island Bridge. I walk up Queen Street, Oliver Bond House, Cook Street and Francis Street. I remember all of my friends and all the good times I had in my youth. I hear of friends that have died and am full of sorrow, but then I remember them in their youth and smile. I feel the warmth when I walk around my beloved Dublin. Paddy and Tony still live there. My father is long dead as is my beloved brother Noel God rest their souls. My mother is still there, very frail but still quite a wit at 96. I meet my old adversaries, men with grown families of their own, and we talk and have a pint. I visit Arron Quay church where were my mother and father were married, John's Lane church were my grandfather said good-bye to Catherine. I hear the church bells ringing, feel the hospitality of my beloved city, recall dear friends living and dead, and I remember "The Rare Old Times."

Also from MX Publishing

The Beekeeper

From Canadian author Bernie Morgan comes the enchanting story of The Beekeeper.

Originally in English the book has been translated into Polish and German already as its appeal crosses the barriers of language and culture.

The Ghost of Crackley Moor

The second illustrated childrens story from Bernie Morgan tells a scary ghost story. Kate, her brothers and a friend discover the secrests and mystery of the wilds of Crackley Moor.

Also from MX Publishing

Portuguese Property Guide

"Contains a great deal of information of interest to potential buyers and people thinking of moving to Portugal"
Destination Algarve

"This book has a great deal of information for anyone looking to buy property in Portugal. It has been well researched to provide the latest information on living and working in the country"
Portugal Magazine

Seeing Spells Achieving

"For anyone with dyslexia, and any parent or someone involved in learning, education and health, these processes of visualisation integrate so well with existing teaching methods and they do give us all another tool, a new choice for growth and development to achieve new goals"

National Family Learning Network

Also from MX Publishing

The Gift – Real Life NLP

"It can be used in so many different ways from helping businesses to giving people the skills they need do better at school, while also being useful for treating phobias and helping people lose weight or stop smoking".
Daily Record

Performance Strategies for Musicians

"If you suffer from stage fright and performance anxiety then help is at hand"
The Pianist Magazine

Also from MX Publishing

Hurghada Property and Egypt's Red Sea Riviera Real Estate

From leading property writer Nick Pendrell comes a comprehensive overview of the Egyptian property market.

Succeed In Sport

Five times British Archery champion Jackie Wilkinson brings us the secrets to enhanced performance across all sports. Contributions from leading Olympians and leading athletes from Athletics, Running, Golf, Karate, Archery, Show Jumping, Cricket and more.

Also from MX Publishing

TOK258 – Morgan Winner at Le Mans

"I would recommend this book to anyone. It is the story of how skill and personal determination can beat the most elaborate, expensive and sophisticated machinery, the story of David versus Goliath. I warmly hope that it inspires the reader to try and achieve their own personal dreams" **Charles Morgan**

Enabled

Born with a disability that confines her to a wheelchair, this is the true story of one woman's dream and her pursuit of it against the odds. Engaging, heart wrenching and compelling are all words that have been used to describe this remarkable book.